Makers of the Supreme Court

First Edition 2016

Makers of the Supreme Court

Keshav Dayal
Senior Advocate

Universal
Law Publishing
an imprint of LexisNexis

This book is a publication of **LexisNexis®**
(A Division of Reed Elsevier India (Pvt) Ltd)
14th floor, Building No 10, Tower–B, DLF Cyber City, Phase-II,
Gurgaon–122002, Haryana, India.
Tel : + 91 124 4774444 Fax: + 91 124 4774100

Website : www.lexisnexis.co.in / E-mail : help.in@lexisnexis.com

Keshav Dayal : *Makers of the Supreme Court,* First Edition, 2016

ISBN: 978-93-5143-740-6

Printed by: Nice Printing Press, Delhi

Printed and bound in India.

Dipak Misra
Judge
Supreme Court of India

10, Tughlak Road
New Delhi-110011
Tel.: 23792196
23792197

FOREWORD

To any serious author, writing a book is an exciting adventure. Some books although appear to be selection of information, they are manifestations of experience with historicity of approach. The author, spreads them before the reader with immense sensibility. Sans sensibility, any book of this nature is nothing but a bunch of papers, may be, sometimes incoherent. Structured and founded on cohesiveness and communicative skill, the book, "The Makers of the Supreme Court", by Mr. Keshav Dayal, even if it deals with historical facts, reads well and in a way, talks to the reader, One is reminded of the saying of Jim Bishop:

> "These are my silent friends. My teachers. My slaves. They sit in mute rows and they have nothing to say unless I ask them. By opening a book, I can make it speak eloquently for as long as I please. The words, the images, the stories, the knowledge, the history, the laughter, the edification, the tears of the world are in my hands."

In the instant book, while the author acquaints the readers with the makers of the Supreme Court of India, the task may sound and appear easy, but a curious thinker will immediately respond by saying that it is not so, for in all possibility, it has not adopted a straight-jacket style of narration of events. It has something in addition to the narration. The intermittent addresses, speeches, reflections, show the keenness of the author to make the reading lively. The book, speaks about an institution which stands for sustaining our organic and vibrant Constitution. The author has anxiously spelt out his purpose in many a way. He takes the reader through the judicial history of India during the British rule, familiarizes him with the discussions in the Constituent Assembly and the ultimate fructification and further impels him to befriend with the great Judges and their views.

The book, "The Makers of the Supreme Court" by Mr. Keshav Dayal is not only informative but enthralling to one who has keen interest to know the history of the highest Court of the country. It is a pearl for the new generation.

Another aspect about the book deserves to be noted. The author devoted certain space with important cases in the early period and also given the biographical sketch of first Judges of the Supreme Court and the first Attorney General. The pains taken to collate and present systematically commends sincere appreciation. The book, keeping the recent developments in view, has discussed about, the establishment of the Supreme Court in the United Kingdom and a brief outline on the appointed Judges to the same. It is, as it seems, to signify the concept of Apex Court in a democratic republic.

The book, I am sure, is bound to satisfy the curiosity of the studious and simultaneously apprise the information seeker to be apprised of the same. It is a beautifully balanced combination of the two. I have no doubt the book shall be an ornament in one's library.

DIPAK MISRA

PREFACE

The Supreme Court of India, the highest court in the country with widest powers has its genesis in the Constitution of India, which was adopted on 26th January, 1950. On this auspicious date the largest and the most honoured institution opened its gates for the Indian people. The mandate of the Constitution as provides in the PREAMBLE *viz.* "justice, social, economic and political, liberty of thought, expression, belief, faith and worship and guaranteeing quality of status and of opportunity", became a reality for the teeming millions of the country men. The story of the Supreme Court emerging form Privy Council to the Federal Court of India is a long and arduous one. The younger generation is unaware of the efforts that have gone into creation of the Supreme Court of India.

1st Part consists of Preface, Gratitude, Foreword and Messages, Notable Quotes and Important Events.

The 2nd Part consists of Judicial Administration during British Period, Role of Privy Council of England and Federal Court of India.

The 3rd Part consists of Independence Era to Inception of Supreme Court, Constitutional Assembly Debates and Role of Constitutional Advisor.

The 4th Part consists of Formation of Supreme Court & 1st sitting, 1st Judges of Supreme Court and 1st Attorney-General, 1st major judgments of Supreme Court, Administration of Supreme Court "Retrospect and Prospect" and Prologue and Epilogue.

The 5th Part consists Biographies of 1st Judges of Supreme Court and 1st Attorney-General and Lighter side of Judges.

Two chapters of Part IV need special mention. The Chapter on the Supreme Court of India "Retrospective and Prospective" is very enlightening and important for the students of law and practicing Advocates, as it gives not only the information about the time of formation of the Supreme Court, but also the latest information on the jurisdiction of the Supreme Court of India, public utilities and facilities, the strength of the Judges and the complete chart of organizational structure of the Supreme Court Registry.

The chapter on Prologue and Epilogue gives information about the formation of the Supreme Court of England and also the biographies of the first judges of the Supreme Court of England. This information is rarely available to any law student and the practicing lawyers at the Supreme Court, and even for the Judges of the superior courts.

It is absolutely necessary to apprise the forthcoming and new generation, including the Law Teachers, members of the Bar and the Bench, about the historical role played by the Supreme Court of India. The various chapters about the creation of the Supreme Court will throw new light, particularly in the minds of the new generation of lawyers.

The book will be relevant and crucial for the present day and future generation of law students, Lawyers and Judiciary.

Keshav Dayal

Keshav Dayal
Senior Advocate

GRATITUDE

The role played by the Indian Constitution-Makers, Constitutional Advisor Shri B.N. Rao, Report of the Constitutional Committee on the Supreme Court in July, 1947, Report of the *Ad-hoc* Committee of the Supreme Court dated May, 1947 and role of Shri Motilal C. Setalvad, first Attorney-General in the Making of the Indian Constitution has been unique and a land mark in the Indian History. However, the present day generation is unaware of the efforts that have gone into making of the present day Supreme Court, which is a model Court not only for the country or the Asian Continent but for the entire world.

The Supreme Court-makers have played a historical role in giving to this country a Supreme Court which is most suitable to the Indian conditions, but which has also drawn considerable inspiration from other world countries including USA, Ireland and the Commonwealth countries.

The inspiration of writing this Book has come from the good response to my earlier books "Reflections of a Lawyer", "Famous Lawyers of Freedom struggle and trial of Freedom Fighters" and "The Makers of the Indian Constitution". The earlier books have won accolades not only from the lawyers and the judges but also from the Cabinet Ministers, Politicians, Governors and most other eminent persons. In fact the present book is a sequel to the book "The Makers of the Indian Constitution".

Various chapters about the making of the Supreme Court throw new lights into the minds of the framers of the Supreme Court who had world-wide vision for the entire country consisting of different cultures and religions. The book also includes the biographies of the First Judges of the Supreme Court including Hon'ble Mr. Justice Harilal Jekisundas Kania, Chief Justice, Hon'ble Sir Syed Fazl Ali, Hon'ble Mr. Justice Mehr Chand Mahajan, Mr. Justice Sudhi Ranjan Das, Mr. Justice Patanjali Shastri and of Shri Motilal C. Setalvad, First Attorney-General of India.

My thanks are due to Shri Anil Kumar Bakshi, Advocate-on-Record, Supreme Court and Solicitor (England & Wales) who has helped me in preparing the chapter on important dates and events as well as the chapter on the Judicial Administration during the British Period and the Role of Privy Council of England and Federal Court in India. He has also been very helpful in looking after the overall preparation of the book. My special thanks are also due to Mr. R.K. Srivastva, Director, Library of the Supreme Court of India and Kumari Meghna Srivastva, B.A. LL.B. (Hons.), who helped me on the Chapter Supreme Court of India – Retrospect and Prospect. This unique chapter in the said book will be very useful for not only to the young Lawyers but also the Advocates practicing in the Supreme Court of India, as the said chapter not only gives the history of the Supreme Court Architectures, Logo of the Supreme Court, History of Federal Court, Supreme Court of India and its present day jurisdiction, the strength of the judges at different times but also the organizational chart of the Supreme Court Registry. I am also thankful to Mr. N.K. Jaggi, Advocates of Jaggi, Attorney at Law for his contribution to the chapter Prologue and Epilogue which gives not only the history of the Supreme Court of England which has been formed much after the formation of the Supreme Court but also the biographies of the first Judges of the Supreme Court of England.

My thanks are also due to many other individuals who have helped me in various ways in completion of the book. I am also thankful to the publisher, Universal Law Publishing Co. Pvt. Ltd, who have always been helpful in publishing my earlier books *viz.* "Reflections of a Lawyer", "Famous Lawyers of Freedom Struggle and Trials of Freedom Fighters" and the "Makers of the Indian Constitution".

I have to place on record my father's life as an ideal lawyer and the image which he carried in the legal profession which has always been a source of unending inspiration for me in all my ventures, including writing the present book.

"I am also thankful to Mr. Prasaran (former Solicitor-General of India) for the speech delivered by him in the Hon'ble Delhi High Court on 29-8-2014."

Keshav Dayal
Senior Advocate

H.L. Dattu
Chief Justice of India

5, Krishna Menon Marg
New Delhi-110011
Tel.: 91-11-23012378 (R)
Telefax: 91-11-23012377

17th December, 2014

MESSAGE

It is a privilege to pen down a message for this book titled "Makers of Supreme Court of India". In a rare detail, the book traverses the history of this Institution from the pre-independence to the contemporary era. It is, indeed, a commendable effort from Shri Keshav Dayal for undertaking this arduous task to commit to paper such untouched aspects of the first Court of this Country.

Over the years of his practice Shri Dayal has earned a distinct reputation in the legal profession that expands well beyond that of being a legal luminary. Hard-work, dedication, consistency and quality are adjectives that are synonymous to Shri Dayal. His status in the fraternity has been cemented as a highly gifted author, and his earlier works such as *"Reflection of a Lawyer"*, *"Famous Lawyers of Freedom Struggle and Trials of Freedom Fighters"* and *"Framing of Indian Constitution and Biographies of the Constitution Makers"* evidence his accomplishments.

The essence of this work is enormous and highly significant for the inquisitive minds of our profession. Shri Dayal has discussed the foundations of the Apex Court that go beyond mere bricks and stones. He has talked of the sacred document-the Constitution of India, the great men and women that walked the corridors of the Court, and the jurists who adorned the noble Bench of the Court.

The history of our Apex Court is indeed extensive and complex. There is a limited scope of resources available to describe the exact chronology and minds behind the Supreme Court of India, and it is only Shri Dayal's passion for the law that could have aided and driven him forward in preparing this book.

I extend my heartfelt appreciation to Shri Dayal for undertaking this challenging task, which will not only serve as a source of knowledge, but also an inspiration to the students of law and practicing advocates.

H.L. Dattu

Justice R.F. Nariman
Judge
Supreme Court of India

4, Teen Murti Marg,
New Delhi-110011

Ph.: 011-23017315
011-23019738

November 25, 2014

MESSAGE

The book is an audacious effort by a distinguished member of the legal fraternity. It delineates the evolution of the Apex Court of the country and very elegantly captures the ethos of the great institution. The author has reflected the legacy of the institution and its makers in a lucid manner. The erudition will make the book an enlightening read for lawyers and the layman alike.

R.F. Nariman

डी वी सदानंद गौड़ा
D.V. Sadananda Gowda

भारत सरकार

मंत्री
कानून एवं न्याय
भारत सरकार
MINISTER
LAW AND JUSTICE
GOVERNMENT OF INDIA

5 Dec., 2014

MESSAGE

I am delighted that Shri Keshav Dayal, Senior Supreme Court Advocate has written the book, *"Makers of Supreme Court of India"*.

Shri Keshav Dayal is a distinguished Senior Advocate of long standing and comes from a family of successful lawyers. His earlier books, *"Famous Lawyers of Freedom Struggle & Trials of Freedom Fighters"*, *"Reflections of a Lawyer"* and *"Framing of the Indian Constitution and Biographies of the Constitution Makers"* were very well received and widely appreciated by the readers. The present book is about the creation of the Supreme Court of India and the historical role played by it.

I expect the book to be widely welcomed by scholars, teachers, lawyers, judges and all enlightened citizens.

My compliments to the author for his endeavours and best wishes for successful publication.

D.V. SADANANDA GOWDA

Shri Keshav Dayal, Sr. Advocate,
209, Lawyers' Chambers,
Delhi High Court,
New Delhi-110003.

Office: 402 'A' Wing, Shastri Bhawan, New Delhi-11001, Tel.: 011-23384567/23386615, Fax : 011-23384241

DELHI HIGH COURT BAR ASSOCIATION

Sher Shah Road, New Delhi-110503 Phones: 011-2338-5562, 2338-5943

Dated: 03/12/2014

MESSAGE

I am happy that Sh. Keshav Dayal, Senior Advocate has written the book, "Makers of the Supreme Court and Biographies of the framers of the Supreme Court".

I know Sh. Keshav Dayal over the years. He has earlier authored three books *viz.* "Reflections of a Lawyer", "Famous Lawyers of Freedom struggle & trials of Freedom Fighters" and "Framing of the Indian Constitution and Biographies of the Constitution Makers" were widely acclaimed by the readers. This book is about the "Makers of the Supreme Court" with useful biographies of the Judges, who were *dramatis personae* in the framing of the Supreme Court.

My best compliments to the author and best wishes for successful publication of the said book.

Rajiv Khosla
President

SUPREME COURT BAR ASSOCIATION (REGD.)

SUPREME COURT OF INDIA, TILAK MARG, NEW DELHI-110001 (INDIA)

Dated 28th Nov., 2014

MESSAGE

I am delighted that Shri Keshav Dayal, Senior Advocate has written the book, "Makers of the Supreme Court and Biographies of the Makers of the Supreme Court.

I have had the privilege to know Shri Keshav Dayal over the years. He is a distinguished Senior Advocate of long standing and comes from a family of successful lawyers. His earlier books "Reflections of a Lawyer", Famous Lawyers of Freedom Struggle & trials of Freedom Fighters" and Framing of the Indian Constitution and Biographies of the Constitution Makers" were well received and widely appreciated by the readers.

It is important for all citizens to understand the working of the Supreme Court. I expect the book to be widely welcomed by Judges, Lawyers, scholars, teachers, and all enlightened citizens interested in understanding the importance of Supreme Court.

My compliments to the author for his endeavours and best wishes for successful publication.

Pravin H. Parekh
President

Phones : **Off.**: 23385903, 23384874 • **Fax**: 23385552 • **Library-1**: 23385551 •**Library-2**: 23384150, 23381762 • **Library-4**: 23385615 • **Ladies Bar**: 23070443 • **Lounge**: 23070449 • **E-mail**: scbaec@gmail.com • **Website**: www.scbaindia.org

R.K.P. Shankardass
Senior Advocate

B-12, MAHARANI BAGH
NEW DELHI- 110065, INDIA
Telephones: 2683 0636, 41627767
Fax: 2684 8104
COURT OFFICE:
87, Lawyers Chambers
Supreme Court of India
New Delhi - 110001
Telephones: 23381041, 23383703
e-mail: rkpslaw@hotmail.com

22 November, 2014

Shri Keshav Dayal
Senior Advocate
Supreme Court and Delhi High Court
New Delhi

Dear Shri Keshav Dayal

We, in the legal profession, are very pleased to see that you are continuing your work of enlightened and objective legal writings, this time on the 'Makers of the Supreme Court of India'. This is an extremely important subject keeping in view the history of the Supreme Court which, over the last half century, has increased in size and made significant changes in approach in dealing with constitutional questions and legal disputes. Your forthcoming contribution will be of great value on this subject.

We have already applauded you on your writings about the role of famous lawyers in the freedom struggle, trials of freedom fighters and, in particular, on your contributions to the framing of the independent Constitution and the great minds which constructed it with such vision, resulting in its continuing acceptance by the people of India since our independence.

We therefore much look forward to the arrival of the new book in the near future and have no doubt it will be equally enlightening and a major contribution to legal jurisprudence.

Yours sincerely

R.K.P. Shankardass
Senior Advocate
President, Bar Association of India

KERALA RAJ BHAVAN
Thiruvananthapuram
Pin: 695 099

25 November, 2014

MESSAGE

I am happy to know that Senior Advocate Shri Keshav Dayal has authored a book titled "Makers of Supreme Court of India" highlighting the historical role played by the Supreme Court of India in the minds of the new generation of lawyers and latest information on the jurisdiction of the Supreme Court of India.

The book, I am glad to note, include chapters on Judicial Administration during British Period, Role of Privy Council of England and Federal Court of India Independence Era to inception of Supreme Court, Constitutional Assembly Debates and Role of Constitutional Advisor, Formation of Supreme Court and 1st sitting, 1st Judges of Supreme Court and 1st Attorney-General, 1st major judgments of Supreme Court, Administration of Supreme Court and Prologue and Epilogue, Biographies of 1st Judges of Supreme Court and 1st Attorney-General and Lighter side of Judges.

I compliment the worthwhile publication and wish the author all success in his future endeavours.

Justice (Retd) P. Sathasivam
Governor of Kerala

Soli J. Sorabjee
To me

MESSAGE

The Supreme Court of our country plays an important role in shaping the life of our nation. Its judgments affect the lives and destiny of millions of our people. Keshav Dayal's book gives an illuminating insight into the makers of Supreme Court of India. And that is done with thoroughness. The book is a must for every consumer of justice as well as victims of injustice.

Soli J. Sorabjee
Former Attorney-General for India

25th November, 2014

भारत सरकार

DR. ABHISHEK MANU SINGHVI
Member of Parliament (Rajya Sabha)
Senior Advocate, Supreme Court of India
Former Additional Solicitor General, India
B.A. (Hons), M.A. (Cantab), Ph.D. (Cantab), PIL (Harvard)

MESSAGE

Mr. Keshav Dayal, one of the senior most advocates practising at the Delhi High Court has always had cerebral interests beyond the mere practice of law. Decades ago, he wrote a book on the law relating to the Delhi Development Authority (DDA). Since then, he has written three more books.

The inclination of practicing lawyers to author books deserves special commendation since the desire, willingness and ability for objective research and felicitous, readable writing is fast dwindling, especially on account of the diverse and pressing exigencies of the profession. Mr. Dayal has always been an exception in this regard, both in his younger days and in the more recent past.

There are very few biographies of the apex court as an institution. This does not pretend to be one but is a valuable contribution to an important subset of that larger theme. Anyone covering a part or the more ambitious whole would be doing yeoman service not only to one-sixth of the planet's population but globally, since the apex Court of India continues to be, indisputably, the most activist in the world and also one wielding, by far, the largest scope of judicial powers.

I, therefore, congratulate the author, wish him many more long years in the service of not only the profession but also legal academia. I look forward to publication of this and more books, especially to the fifth part of this book, since I am a student of biographies.

ABHISHEK SINGHVI

NOTABLE QUOTES

(1) "The writ of this Court will run over territory extending to over two million square miles inhabited by a population of about 330 million. It can truly be said that the jurisdiction and powers of this Court, in their nature and extent, are wider than those exercised by the highest Court of any country in the Commonwealth or by the Supreme Court of the United States".

(Inaugural address by Shri Motilal C. Setalvad, Attorney-General of India on opening of the Supreme Court of India on 28th January, 1950)

(2) "The role which the court will be called upon to play in mediating between the individual and the Government. The detailed enumeration of fundamental rights in the Constitution and the provisions which enable them to be reasonably restricted will need wise and discriminating decisions. On the Court will fall the delicate and difficult task of ensuring to the citizen the enjoyment of his guaranteed rights consistently with the rights of the society and the State".

(Inaugural address by Shri Motilal C. Setalvad, Attorney-General of India on opening of the Supreme Court of India on 28th January, 1950)

(3) "We at the Bar have confidence that the Supreme Court of India, which is being inaugurated today, will, in course of time, attain the same judicial eminence, and that memorable and epoch-making judgments will illumine its records. The task before us all is the building of a nation alive to its national and international duties, consisting of a strong Central Authority and federated units each possessed of ample power for the diverse uses of a progressive people. In the attainment of this noble end, we hope and trust that this court will play a great and singular role and establish itself in the consciousness of the Indian people. 'Like all human institutions, the Supreme Court,' we hope, will earn reverence through truth".

(Concluding address by Shri Motilal C. Setalvad, Attorney-General of India on opening of the Supreme Court of India on 28th January, 1950)

(4) "The duty of interpreting that Constitution with an enlightened liberality falls on the Supreme Court. The Supreme Court will declare and interpret the law of the land, and, with the high traditions behind the Judiciary of this country, we are convinced that the work will be done in no spirit of formal or barren legalism. It will be our endeavour to interpret the Constitution, not as a rigid body, but, as a living organism, having within itself the force and power of self-government. We trust, that, in doing so, we shall allow the constitutional usages and conventions recognized in all civilized independent countries to be respected. The Supreme Court, however, under the colour of interpretation, cannot alter or amend the law. But, within the limits prescribed, we are quite sure that the Supreme Court will be able to make a substantial contribution towards the formation of India into a great unit retaining its own civilization, traditions and customs. With the establishment of the Supreme Court of India, we shall develop our own jurisprudence based on our historical background and we trust that that will be an important and useful contribution to the creation of International Law. The Federal Court, as interpreting the Constitution of the country, had earned the confidence of the country. In endowing the Supreme Court of India with very wide powers, the Constituent Assembly – the Assembly representing the voice of the people through its elected representatives- has shown complete confidence in the Court as the final body for dispensing justice between individuals and also between States and States, and the States and the Centre. We hope to deserve that confidence. We trust that the people of India will also maintain the independence, honour and dignity of the Supreme Court".

(Speech by Hon'ble Sir Harilal Jekisundas Kania, Chief Justice of India on opening of the Supreme Court of India on 28th January, 1950)

(5) "The Indian Bar has maintained the high tradition of the profession. Different conditions in different provinces have so far prevented the creation of one Bar with one good reliable standards of advocacy, knowledge and etiquette. With the

inauguration of the Independent Republic of India and the States, Union Courts attaining the status of the States High Courts, one can look forward in time to the existence of one Bar for India, with a very high standard of efficiency to assist the Courts in the administration of justice".

(Speech by Hon'ble Sir Harilal Jekisundas Kania, Chief Justice of India on opening of the Supreme Court of India on 28th January, 1950)

(6) "The Supreme Court, an all-India Court will stand firm and aloof from party politics and political theories. It is unconcerned with the changes in the Government. The Court stands to administer the law for the time being in force, has goodwill and sympathy for all, but is allied to none. Occupying that position, we hope and trust it will play a great part in the building-up of the nation, and in stabilizing the roots of civilization which have twice been threatened and shaken by two world wars, and maintain the fundamental principles of justice which are the emblem of God"

(Concluding Speech by Hon'ble Sir Harilal Jekisundas Kania, Chief Justice of India on opening of the Supreme Court of India on 28th January, 1950)

(7) "It is satisfactory to think that, notwithstanding all the difficulties of the day, we are all determined to maintain and strengthen the rule of law, and I feel quite confident that the Supreme Court of India will prove an effective instrumental for this end. I like to think that you share with us common traditions and I feel sure that we shall each gain strength and wisdom from the development of each other's jurisprudence".

(Message from the Lord Chancellor of England read by Hon'ble Sir Harilal Jekisundas Kania, Chief Justice of India on opening of the Supreme Court of India on 28th January, 1950)

(8) "The courts are not at liberty to declare an Act void because in their opinion it is opposed to a spirit supposed to pervade the Constitution but not expressed in words. Where the fundamental law has not limited, either in terms or by necessary implication, the general powers conferred upon the Legislature we cannot declare a limitation under the notion of having discovered something in the spirit of the Constitution which is

not even mentioned in the instrument. It is difficult upon any general principles to limit the omni-potence of the sovereign legislative power by judicial interposition, except so far as the express words of a written Constitution give that authority. It is also stated, if the words be positive and without ambiguity".

[Argument put by the first Attorney-General of India on the hearing of the first case of *A.K. Gopalan* v. *The State of Madras,* 1950 SCR 88].

(9) "that the legislature had a wide field of choice in determining and classifying the subject of its laws, and if the law dealt alike with all of a certain class, it was normally not open to the charge of denial of equal protection. But the classification could not be arbitrary. To be valid, it had necessarily to rest upon some real and substantial distinction bearing a reasonable and just relation to the things in respect of which the classification was made".

[Judgment in the case of *Chiranjit Lal Chouhan* v. *Union of India,* 1950 SCR 869].

CONTENTS

PART XI

TABLE OF CASES

PART I

IMPORTANT EVENTS

31-12-1600. East India Company incorporated in England under a charter granted by Queen Elizabeth. Managed by Court of Directors (1 Governor and 24 Directors). The Company Court could make laws, ordinances etc., and set penalties and was instrumental in setting up new legal system in India.

1672. First British court established in India at Bombay by Governor Gerald Aungier.

1726. Charter issued by King George I for introduction of English law selectively by establishment of Mayor's (Crown) Courts in India. Against decision of Mayor's Court appeal lay to the Governor-in-Council and thereafter, in certain cases, appeal lay to King-in Council (later called The Privy Council) in England.

1774. Supreme Court for Calcutta replaced the Mayor's Court at Calcutta under The Regulating Act, 1773 and Sir Impey was appointed as the Chief Justice alongwith three other Judges. Appeal against Supreme Court, in civil cases of high values, could be filed before King-in-Council. In criminal cases appeal to King-in-Council could be filed only through Supreme Court.

1800. Supreme Court for Madras was established at Madras against whose order appeal lay to the Privy Council.

1823. Supreme Court was established at Bombay against whose order appeal lay to the Privy Council.

1833. England enacted Judicial Committee Act providing for the reorganization of the Privy Council. A committee of the King's Council called the "Judicial Committee of the Privy Council" was constituted consisting of the president of the Privy Council and other members and it took the shape of The highest Court of Justice. However, it only gave "advice" in recommendatory form to His majesty which, in practice was always followed.

Till 1857. Two types of judicial systems were prevalent. Supreme Courts were the Royal Courts and Sadar Diwani Adalats were the Company Courts in India.

1857. Indian war of Independence took place forcing many changes in the Royal judicial system for India.

1858. East India Company's Government was replaced by direct rule of Crown of England. Dual system of King's Courts and Company's Courts came to an end through Government of India Act, 1858.

1862. By Indian High Courts Act, 1862, High Courts (courts of highest appeal in India) replaced Supreme Courts for Calcutta, Madras and Bombay. Original jurisdiction was bestowed upon the three High Courts in the presidency towns of Bombay, Madras and Calcutta.

17-3-1868. High Court was established at Agra under The Indian High Courts Act, 1862.

1875. High Court at Agra was shifted to Allahabad.

1915. Government of India Act passed putting restrictions on the High Courts for Calcutta, Madras and Bombay.

1915. Judicial Committee of Privy Council, England consisted of one division exclusively for appeals from India.

Feb. 1916. High Court established at Patna.

March 1919 High Court established at Lahore by raising the status of Punjab Chief Court.

1928.	Motilal Nehru report suggested creation of Supreme Court at the apex of Indian Judiciary.
1932.	The legislative Assembly accepted resolution recommending establishment of a Supreme Court of India.
1935.	Government of India Act passed bringing High Courts under Provincial Governments.
Jan. 1936.	High Court established at Nagpur.
6-12-1937.	A Federal Court for India was established at Delhi for constitutional matters only. Appeal against its decisions could go before the Privy Council. The British Government exercised administrative control over the Federal Court.
1947.	India gained independence.
1948.	Federal Court curtailed the jurisdiction of the Privy Council, England.
10-10-1949.	Jurisdiction of Privy Council, England was abolished.
19-12-1949.	Privy Council England disposed of last appeal from India.
26-1-1950.	Supreme Court of India established as Court of last resort. The Federal Court stood abolished with effect from this date. Judges of the Federal Court became Judges of the Supreme Court of India and all cases pending before the Federal Court stood transferred to the Supreme Court of India.
28-1-1950.	First sitting (inaugural session) of Supreme Court of India.

PART II

JUDICIAL ADMINISTRATION DURING BRITISH PERIOD, ROLE OF PRIVY COUNCIL OF ENGLAND AND FEDERAL COURT IN INDIA

CHAPTER I

JUDICIAL ADMINISTRATION DURING BRITISH PERIOD

After the Norman conquest of England in 1066, the King-in-Council (also known as the Privy Council) came to be regarded as the court of last resort throughout his realm in case of default, defects, or miscarriage of justice perpetrated in the lower courts.

The Mayor's Court at Calcutta gave place to the Supreme Court for Calcutta in 1774. The Regulating Act, 1773, provided for a right of appeal to the King-in-Council from the decisions of the Supreme Court for Calcutta by any person thinking himself aggrieved by any judgment or determination of the Supreme Court for Calcutta.

The Mayor's Court at Madras and Bombay gave place to the Recorders' Court in 1797. In 1800, the Recorder's Court at Madras gave place to the Supreme Court for Madras. Recorder's Court at Bombay gave place to the Supreme Court for Bombay in 1823.

In 1802, the Sadar Diwani Adalat was established at Madras. In 1818, the Sadar Diwani Adalat at Calcutta relinquished the authority to hear appeals from the Sadar Diwani Adalat at Madras and provisions were made for taking appeals from the Madras Adalat to the King-in-Council.

In Bombay, the right to appeal to the Privy Council was allowed as early as in 1812.

The Act of 1833 had provided for the appointment of two retired Indian Judges as assessors to the Judicial Committee Privy Council.

An Order-in-Council, dated the 10th April, 1838, was enacted in pursuance of the Act of 1833 which provided that after the 31st day of December, 1838, no appeal to Her Majesty-in-Council should be allowed by any Supreme Court in India, or by any Sadar Diwani Adalat, unless the petition for that purpose was presented within six months from the date of the Judgment,

The next important provision made by Parliament to regulate appeals to the Privy Council from India was in 1845, when an Act, was passed to amend the previous Act of 1833.

With the creation of the three High Courts in 1861, a major change occurred in the scheme of judicial institutions in India. The erstwhile Sadar Adalats and Supreme Courts for Calcutta, Madras and Bombay came to an end, and an appeal could be made to the Privy Council.

Appeals could be taken to the Privy Council not only from the final judgment or decrees of the High Courts but also from interlocutory orders. The High Court in its discretion could grant permission to appeal to the Privy Council from any preliminary or interlocutory judgment, decree or order or sentence in any proceeding not being of a criminal nature. In criminal cases, appeals could lie to the Privy Council from any judgment or sentence of High Court made in exercise of its original jurisdiction, or in any case where a point of law had been reserved for the opinion of the High Court by another court of original jurisdiction.

The Civil Procedure Code, enacted subsequently, also laid down more or less similar provisions regulating appeals to the Privy Council from the Indian High Courts.

Even when the royal charter or legislation laid down the conditions under which appeals 'as of right' were permitted to the Privy Council, it did not necessarily exhaust the whole ambit of the Crown's prerogative as the fountain of justice. Usually, the King-in-Council specifically reserved to itself, by making a suitable provision in the concerned Charter or the Act, the power to grant special leave to appeal in those cases which did not qualify to come before him 'as of right' under the conditions stipulated.

After 1862, the Charters of the High Courts gave a very restricted right of appeal to the Privy Council from the High Courts' decisions in criminal matters.

CHAPTER II
ROLE OF PRIVY COUNCIL OF ENGLAND

As a judicial institution, the Privy Council was unique and unparalleled among the courts of the world. The range of jurisdiction was extremely broad as it heard appeals from many dominions, colonies and plantations. Within its scope and ambit, the Judicial Committee embraced the legal interests of nearly one-fifth of the human race. It was concerned with almost every known system of jurisprudence with judicial institutions of every type, and with every kind of dispute. By the Act of 1833 and the later legislation, the Privy Council had been transformed into a great Imperial court with unimpeachable authority. The responsibility of exercising such a vast jurisdiction was always an onerous one. It was undertaken by very eminent lawyers. As a rule, the Privy Council was composed of persons who, on account of their political experience, legal learning and professional eminence were eminently qualified for that heavy duty and difficult trust. In spite of the fact that the Judicial Committee was called upon to administer a variety of different systems of law, with some of which none of its members was personally conversant, there has been very little criticism of the quality of its decisions. This achievement was made possible because the members of the Judicial Committee possessed a wide knowledge of law and had a rare insight into the issues involved in the controversies which came before them for decision.

In course of time the jurisdiction of the Privy Council in case-law and equity arising in England was abolished. Petitions in relation of the causes decided by the courts in England came to be brought before the King-in-Parliament. Thus, originated the modern judicial function of the House of Lords to correct the errors of the lower courts in England. The House of Lords was the final court of appeal from the courts in England. For the British possessions beyond the seas, petitions seeking justice continued to go to the King-in-Council which functioned throughout as the court of last resort and as an ultimate court of appeal for such territories.

As the overseas colonies of England grew and developed from the 17th century onwards, Privy Council's judicial function assumed great importance. As regards the courts in India, the Privy Council, or the Judicial Committee of the Privy Council (JCPC), as it came to be called officially after 1833, acted as the highest court of appeal for over two centuries. It made a great contribution towards establishing a high standard of justice in the country and creation and ascertainment of law and, therefore, the Privy Council occupies a unique place in the Indian Legal History.

In 1726, for the first time a right to appeal to the King-in-Council was granted from the courts in India and first case from India was heard by the Privy Council.

From the Imperial point of view, the advantages of the system of appeal to the Privy Council were many. It was through this body that the common law of England was introduced into all the dominions and colonies under the British rule as the bases of their legal systems. Through it, a common view of the principles of the common law and legal issues was enforced throughout the length and breadth of the Empire wherever the common law happened to prevail. It enforced a true and uniform interpretation of the royal prerogative throughout the Empire. Many Acts enacted by the Imperial Parliament were adopted by the Dominions or were made applicable there. The Privy Council enforced uniformity of interpretation of such Acts. This influence of the Board was really of great value for otherwise there would have been inevitably a great divergence between the different parts of the Empire in construing the same statutes. Thus, the Privy Council maintained a uniformity of common law doctrines throughout the length and breadth of the Empire. The Judicial Committee always insisted on the maintenance of the highest standards of justice and judicial procedure, specially in the field of criminal justice. Its insistence on maintenance of basic principles of fair procedure, especially in the field of criminal justice did certainly help the nascent colonies in developing their judicial administration on sound lines.

The Judicial Committee Privy Council rendered a great and meritorious service to the Indian legal system. Its association with the Indian legal system subsisted for nearly two hundred years. It started at time when the British system of justice was in its formative stages in India-when justice was administered by law judges without any definite and certain body of law to guide them. In the days when confusion in the field of substantive law was great, and legislative activity negligible, the Privy Council set itself to the task of ascertaining the law, formulating and setting legal principles, moulding and shaping them. It was through the Privy Council that the introduction of the common law into India was encouraged and stimulated. Its association with Indian judicature affected the latter in a very profound manner. The Privy Council, as noted above, consisted of senior judges of England having a firm grounding and thorough training in the English law. It was but natural that when such persons constituted the ultimate court of appeal, they would, wherever possible, introduce their own notions of justice into the Indian legal system. This was what actually happened. "Justice, equity and good conscience" which the Company's Judicature was required to apply in the absence of a specific rule of law, came to be regarded as the basis to introduce English law into the mofussil of India and the trend became all the more accentuated with the activation of the Privy Council. It acted as a channel through which English legal concepts came to be assimilated with the body and fabric of the Indian law. It served as bridge between the Indian and English legal systems over which legal ideas travelled from England to India. In course of time, English common law came to be accepted, openly and avowedly, as the basis of codification of law in India, and its final interpretation by the Privy Council in the light of the latest developments in the field of English common law was very helpful for the development of the Indian law.

K.M. Munshi, the great Parliamentarian observed as such:

> The British Parliament and the Privy Council are the two great institutions which the Anglo-Saxon race has given to mankind. The Privy Council during the last few centuries has not only laid down law, but co-ordinated the concept of right and obligations throughout all the Dominions and Colonies in British Commonwealth. So far as India is

concerned, the role of the Privy Council has been one of the most important. It has been a great unifying force and for us Indians it became the instrument and embodiment of the rule of law, a concept on which alone we have based the democratic institutions which we have set-up in our Constitution.

At a time when there was no link between the various Sadar Adalats, Supreme Courts, and then the High Courts in India, and when they could interpret the law differently from one another, the Privy Council provided an unifying force, a connecting link, between them.

The Privy Council thus, enjoyed a great reputation in India for its integrity and impartiality as a judicial institution which placed it in a category apart from other colonial institutions.

CHAPTER III

ESTABLISHMENT OF FEDERAL COURT AND PRE-INDEPENDENCE ERA

In spite of many advantages to the Indian Legal System flowing from the practice of appeals from India going to the Privy Council, the system suffered from a few drawbacks as well. The Judicial Committee situated as it was in London, at a distance of 5,000 miles away from India, worked under certain obvious handicaps. It was constituted primarily of the British Judges, many of whom had no intimate personal knowledge of the Indian conditions and manners. The absence of knowledge about the local conditions in India was unquestionably a disadvantage both to the Court and to the counsel who had to be engaged in England. Being remote from India the Judicial Committee was insufficiently in touch with the Indian life and, consequently, it could not always appreciate the Indian point of view. Due to distant location the Judicial Committee made the disposal of appeals very dilatory and expensive.

The process of taking appeals to the Privy Council came to be regarded as casting a reflection and an aspersion on the competency, capacity and integrity of the Indian lawyers and Judges. The question was rather one of national honour and prestige. The nationalist public opinion desired an Indian Court manned by Indians for Indians.

In 1928, the Motilal Nehru Report envisaged a federal constitution for India. It suggested the creation of a Supreme Court at the apex of the Indian judiciary, which would take over the appellate work of the Privy Council.

The idea of accepting a Federal Court as part of the proposed federal polity in India was found acceptable at the Second Round Table Conference held in London. The idea of a Supreme Court was also generally acceptable though there was difference of opinion as regards the jurisdiction of such a Court. The Legislative Assembly in India also accepted a resolution in 1932 recommending the establishment of a 'Supreme Court of India'. When the final session of the Round Table Conference met in 1932, there arose a difference of opinion on the question "whether there should be a Federal Court as apart from a Supreme Court or whether there should be a Supreme Court as well".

In 1933, British Government issued a White Paper setting out its proposals for constitutional reform in India. The White Paper envisaged a federal set-up in India and, as consequence thereof, contained a proposal for establishment of Federal Court having original jurisdiction to decide disputes between the Centre and the States and the States *inter se* and in its appellate jurisdiction to hear all matters concerned with the interpretation of the proposed constitution. There was to be an appeal to the Privy Council from the Federal Court.

The White Paper also envisaged the possibility of setting-up of a separate Supreme Court to hear appeals from the High Courts in other matters not involving issues of Constitutional law. The Supreme Court would in general, replace the Privy Council, except that certain appeals could still be allowed to the Judicial Committee. Accordingly, the Government of India Act, 1935, provided only for the establishment of Federal Court.

The present-day Supreme Court of India is the culmination of the evolutionary process which started with creation of the Federal Court of India in 1937. The Government of India Act 1935, sought to inaugurate a federal polity in India.

The Act of 1935 made provisions to establish a Federal Court in India. The Court was formally inaugurated on the 1st October, 1937.

The first judges of the Court: Sir Maurice Gwyer (Chief Justice); and two *puisine* judges, Sir Shah Muhammad Sulaiman, and M.R. Jayakar. The Court held its first sitting at Delhi on December 6, 1937.

Appeals could go to the Privy Council from any judgment rendered by the Federal Court in the exercise of its original jurisdiction, and, in any other case, by leave of the Federal Court or of the King-in-Council.

Government of India Act, 1935, empowered the Federal Parliament in India, with the pervious sanction of the Governor-General, to enact legislation for the appellate jurisdiction of the Federal Court within certain limits, and consequently, to abolish appeals to the Privy Council to that extent.

It was confined only to constitutional controversies and there were not many such cases under the Government of India Act, 1935. The Court thus sat only for few days each year. It had no jurisdiction to decide private law disputes or cases under the criminal law. In such matters, appeals continued to go direct to the Privy Council from the High Courts. The immediate effect of establishing the Federal Court was to increase rather than diminish, the number of appeals to the Privy Council, because the decisions handed down by the Federal Court were themselves subject to appeal to the Privy Council.

During the period 1937 to 1947, several unsuccessful attempts were made in the Indian Legislature to extend the jurisdiction of the Federal Court, but these attempts failed because of the "intransigence of the colonial rulers which provided the principal obstacle to any extension of the appellate jurisdiction of the Federal Court."

PART III

INDEPENDENCE ERA TO INCEPTION OF SUPREME COURT, CONSTITUTIONAL ASSEMBLY DEBATES AND QUESTIONNAIRE OF CONSTITUTIONAL ADVISOR

CHAPTER I

POST-INDEPENDENCE ERA TO INCEPTION OF SUPREME COURT OF INDIA

Things changed however, after 1947 as a result of the change in the constitutional status of the country.

On January 26, 1950, the Supreme Court of India came into existence under the new Constitution. During the interim period from 1947 to 1950, certain preliminary steps had to be taken with a view to eventual abolition of appeals to the Privy Council. The first step in this direction was taken by the Central Legislature in 1948 when it enacted the Federal Court (Enlargement of Jurisdiction) Act I of 1948 to provide for the enlargement of the appellate jurisdiction of the Federal Court so as to embrace civil appeals from the High Courts, and, correspondingly, to restrict any direct appeals to the Privy Council. Under the Act, appeals were to lie to the Federal Court from any judgment of a High Court.

Henceforth, no direct appeal was to lie to the Privy Council either with or without special leave, from any such judgment. The Act of 1948 did not completely abolish appeals to the Privy Council. It did not touch appeals in criminal cases. Appeals to the Privy Council in civil cases or constitutional cases were still possible by leave of the Federal Court or the King-in-Council.

This Act therefore did not completely sever India's ties with Privy Council. It did not completely abolish appeal to Privy Council.

Final step to abolish the Privy Council's jurisdiction was taken in 1949. In September, 1949, about 70 civil appeals and 10 criminal appeals were pending before the Privy Council from India. Before January 26, 1950, the Privy Council was expected to dispose of a few of these pending appeals leaving some still in the balance. In anticipation of the new Constitution, the Indian Constituent Assembly passed the Abolition of Privy Council Jurisdiction Act on the 24th September, 1949, to abolish the jurisdiction of the Privy Council in respect of appeals from India and also to provide for pending appeals so that there might be minimum trouble and inconvenience of the date of the commencement of the new Constitution, and the process of transition might be smoothened. The Act came into force on the 10th October, 1949.

The Act abolished the jurisdiction of His Majesty-in-Council to entertain appeals and petitions from any judgment, decree or order of any Court or Tribunal in India, including appeals and petitions in criminal matters, whether the Privy Council exercised such jurisdiction by virtue of the royal prerogative or otherwise. All pending appeals excepting those which the Privy Council could dispose of before the inauguration of the new Constitution, were to stand transferred to the Federal Court.

The last appeal from India was disposed of by the Privy Council on December 15, 1949 and with this came to an end India's 200- year-old connection with Privy Council.

On January 26, 1950, the Federal Court gave way to the Supreme Court under the new Constitution, and thus began an exciting new era in Indian Legal History. The Court was inaugurated on January 28, 1950.

CHAPTER II

SOME IMPORTANT QUESTIONS RAISED REGARDING FORMATION AND FUNCTIONING OF THE SUPREME COURT IN THE CONSTITUENT ASSEMBLY DEBATES

Some important and interesting questions regarding the formation and functioning of the Supreme Court rose in the

Constituent Assembly during the discussions on the draft Constitution. Draft articles 103 to 122 of the draft Constitution were discussed in the Constituent Assembly. The makers of the Constitution were fully alive to the important role which the Supreme Court was to play in the Indian History. Some of the important aspects discussed in the Constituent Assembly are given below:—

1. Whether there should be a minimum age prescribed for the appointment of Supreme Court Judges. R. Pattabhi Sitaramayya and others wanted a new sub-clause to be inserted in article 103 prescribing that there should be a minimum age for the appointment of Supreme Court Judge as 55 years. This amendment, if introduced would debar persons of outstanding merit, who are less than 55 years of age, as pointed out in The Framing of India's Constitution (Vol. IV) by B. Shiva Rao that "it would be better to leave this question to the President to decide about the experience and mature understanding of the intended candidate".
2. It was suggested by Pattabhi Sitaramayya, Smt. G. Durgabai, Thakurdas Bhargava, B.V. Keskar, T.T. Krishnamachari, M. Ananthasayanam Ayyangar and K. Santhanam that the amendment be made to clause 7 of article 103 which would prevent a retired Judge of the Supreme Court from being appointed as the Chairman of an Inquiry Commission or to other similar offices. This debate also pointed out the problem being faced in the appointments of Supreme Court Judges to a large number of Inquiry Commissions and similar other offices, which sometimes questions the role of the Supreme Court Judges in holding such offices.
3. Tajamul Hussain wanted an amendment to sub-clause 2 of article 103 which would dispense with consultation with any of the judges of the High Courts in the States. The amendment would make consultations with all the Judges of the Supreme Court obligatory, and to dispense with consultation with any of the judges of High Courts in the States. Consultation with judges of the High Courts in States especially with the Chief Justice of a High Court would certainly be useful before appointing a judge or an advocate of the High Court as Judge of the Supreme Court.

4. Chief Justice (Mr. Mallik) of Allahabad High Court suggested that all the Chief Justices of the High Courts of States should be *ex-officio,* judges of the Supreme Court and a provision to that effect should be included in the Constitution. There is a similar provision in the Judicature Act, 1873 under which the Chief Justices of the various divisions are *ex-officio* judges of the Court of Appeal in England. It is submitted that this analogy would hardly be applicable and workable for the Supreme Court of India.
5. There was a suggestion in amending article 103(1) in view of the views of the Federal Court and the Chief Justices of the Provincial High Courts why a minimum number of Judges to be appointed to the Supreme Court should be prescribed by the Constitution and the number should be left to be determined from time to time according to the volume of the work coming to the Court. It is felt that the Constitution has rightly suggested a minimum number of Judges *viz.* 7 in the draft Constitution, which could be increased in case of work in the Supreme Court.
6. It was also suggested that under articles 103(3) and 193(2), provisions may be inserted to the effect that any person should not be appointed as Judge of the Supreme Court or of a High Court, who has at any point of time accepted a post of a Minister in the Union of India or in other State.This was intended to prevent a person who had accepted office of Minister, exercising his influence in order to become a Judge at any time. As per the views of Mr. V. Shiva Rao "it is unnecessary to put these prohibitions into the Constitution. The Attorney-General in England is invariably one of the Ministers of the Crown and often even a Cabinet Minister; he is often appointed a Judge afterwards (The Lord Chancellor is, of course, both a Cabinet Minister and the head of the Judiciary). In India, Sapru and Sircar were Law Members, or Law Ministers as they would be called in future; no one would suggest that men of this type should be ineligible for appointment as Judges afterwards".

   It is submitted that merit alone should be the criteria for this highest court and no constitutional prohibition should stand in the way of merit if recognised.

7. There was a suggestion of changes to be made in sub-clause (b) of clause (3) of article 103 by the Editor of the Indian Law Review and some other members of the Calcutta Bar who have pointed out that the recruitment to the judiciary should only be made from practicing lawyers. It is felt that this would be restricting the appointment of Judges from practicing lawyers only, and the proposed system was fair and beneficial for the working of the highest court of the land.
8. There was a suggestion from A.B. Rudra (Principal Jaipuria College of Kolkata) for making changes in clause (3) of article 103, that a new article should be inserted in this clause to make a new category for the appointment in the Supreme Court *viz.*, distinguished jurists etc. It was suggested that for a wider choice also, it is desirable to have one or two distinguished persons of outstanding legal background and juristic learning to be considered for the appointment as a Judge, and which is not necessarily confined to judges and advocates, and he suggested the addition of this new provision which is based on a similar provision in the statute of the International Court of Justice.
9. In Article 107 it was suggested by R.K. Sidhwa that article 107 be deleted so that the employment of retired judges in the Supreme Court may be all together stopped. It is suggested that the same is included in the provision and the services of the retired judges which can be suitably used as and when need arises by the Chief Justice of the Supreme Court.
10. Power of the President to consult Supreme Court

    With respect to article 119 (Power of the President to Consult Supreme Court), the Editor of the Indian Law Review and some other members of the Calcutta Bar expressed the view that article 119 should be deleted for the following reasons:—

    "while appreciating the utility of a provision like this for prompt dispatch of official business, it appears to us undesirable that the Supreme Court will at the behest of the executive express views on hypothetical questions extra-judicially. This, in effect, implies a sort of legislative power.

Pronouncement by the Supreme Court in such cases must necessarily be a stumbling block to the litigants later on seeking adjudication on those issues while the opinion itself has been reached without the assistance of the counsel of the parties. The American method of limiting the jurisdiction only to justiciable issues, "cases" and/or "controversies" is not only adequate but also preferable. We feel that law officers of the Government are quite competent to guide the executive in this matter.

It may be pointed out that article 119 followed the recommendations of the *ad hoc* Committee of Supreme Court about the advisory jurisdiction of such court which has been adopted by the Constituent Assembly, **(please refer to paragraph 11 of the Report of the *ad-hoc* committee as in Appendix)**

11. With respect to the powers of the Supreme Court to frame rules, the Bihar Lawyers' conference at its 4th session of Gaya suggested that clause (1) of article 121 the words " with the approval of the President" be deleted. It may be pointed out that this amendment involves a question of policy. Clause (1) of article 121 follows sub-section (1) of section 214 of the Government of India Act, 1935, in which the words "with the approval of the Governor-General" occur. The Federal Court judges and the Chief Justice of the Provincial High Courts have not objected to the retention of the words "with the approval of the President" in that clause.

    The Bihar Lawyers' conference also proposed that there should be no restriction in the time to be allowed to the advocates to make their submissions. In the said rules, the drafting Committee and the Chief Justice and the Judges of the Calcutta High Court also recommended that the words ("and the time to be allowed to the Advocates etc." in article 121 be deleted).

12. Regarding power of every Judge of the Supreme Court to sit for the purpose of deciding any case involving a substantial question of law as to the interpretation of the Constitution or for the purpose of hearing any reference. The Hon'ble Chief Justice and judges of the Calcutta High Court also desire to point out that the proviso to article 121(2) as drafted seems to suggest that each individual judge will decide whether

he will sit or not, and are of opinion that if the intention be that each judge, unless he is unable to sit owing to illness, personal interest or other sufficient cause, shall sit, the proviso may be amended to make the meaning clear".

The Drafting Committee, October, 1948 proposed that for the proviso to clause (2) of article 121, the following be substituted:

Provided that it shall be the duty of every Judge to sit for the said purposes unless owing to illness he is unable to do so, or owing to personal interest or other sufficient cause considers that he ought not to do so.

Note.—This amendment was intended to meet the point raised by the judges of the Calcutta High Court with regard to the proviso to clause (2) of article 121 without creating the difficulty envisaged in this regard.

CHAPTER III

REPORT OF THE *AD HOC* COMMITTEE ON THE SUPREME COURT MAY 21, 1947 BY S. VARADACHARIAR, A. KRISHNASWAMI AYYAR, B.L. MITTER, K.M. MUNSHI AND B.N. RAU

We, the undersigned, members of the committee appointed to consider the constitution and powers of the Supreme Court have the honour to submit this Court Report.

2. We considered the question under the following heads:

I. Jurisdiction and powers of the Supreme Court.

II. Advisory jurisdiction of the court.

III. Ancillary powers of the court.

IV. Constitution and strength of the Court.

V. Qualifications and mode of appointment of judges.

VI. Tenure of office and conditions of service of judges.

I. Jurisdiction and Powers of the Supreme Court

3. A Supreme Court with jurisdiction to decide upon the constitutional validity of Acts and laws can be regarded as a necessary implication of any federal scheme. This jurisdiction

need not however belong exclusively to the Supreme Court. Even under the existing Indian Constitution, the question of the validity of Acts and laws is permitted to be raised in any court whenever that question arises in a litigation before that court.

4. A Supreme Court for certain purposes being thus a necessity, we consider that the court may well be given the following additional powers under the new Indian Constitution:

(a) Exclusive jurisdiction in disputes between the Union and a unit or between one unit and another.

5. The Supreme Court is the best available forum for the adjudication of such disputes, and its jurisdiction should be exclusive.

(b) Jurisdiction with respect to Matters arising out of Treaties made by the Union.

6. The treaty-making power belongs to the Union as part of the subject of the Union, 'Foreign Affairs. It would, therefore, be appropriate to invest the Supreme Court of the Union with jurisdiction to decide finally, though not necessarily in the first instance, upon all matters arising out of treaties including extradition between the Union and a foreign State. At this stage we do not deal with inter-unit extradition, because this will depend upon the ultimate distribution of powers between the Union and the Units.

(c) Jurisdiction in respect of Such Other Matters within the Competence of the Union as the Union Legislature may prescribe.

7. If the Union Legislature is competent to legislate on a certain matter, it is obviously competent to confer judicial power in respect of that matter on a Tribunal of its own choice, and if it chooses the Supreme Court for the purpose, the Court will have the jurisdiction so conferred.

(d) Jurisdiction for the Purpose of Enforcing the Fundamental Rights guaranteed by the Constitution.

8. Clause 22 of the draft of the fundamental rights provided that the right to move the Supreme Court by appropriate proceedings for the enforcement of fundamental rights is guaranteed. We think, however, that it is undesirable to make

the jurisdiction of the Supreme Court in such matters exclusive. The citizen will practically be denied these fundamental rights if, whenever they are violated, he is compelled to seek the assistance of the Supreme Court as the only court from which he can obtain redress. Where there is no other court with the necessary jurisdiction, the Supreme Court should have it; where there is some other court with the necessary jurisdiction, the Supreme Court should have appellate jurisdiction, including powers of revision.

(e) General Appellate Jurisdiction similar to that now exercised by the Privy Council.

9. Under the new Constitution the jurisdiction of the Privy Council as the ultimate appellate authority will disappear and it is obviously desirable that a similar jurisdiction should now be conferred on the Supreme Court. So far as the British Indian units are concerned, this jurisdiction should be co-extensive with the present jurisdiction of the Privy Council. As regards the Indian State units, there are at least two classes of cases where, in the interests of uniformity, it is clearly desirable that the final decision should rest with the Supreme Court, namely—

(1) cases involving the interpretation of law of the Union, and

(2) Cases involving the interpretation of a law of a unit other than the State concerned.

Sir B.L. Mitter suggests that such uniformity can be obtained either by invoking the appellate authority of the Supreme Court or by a reference of the particular issue to the Supreme Court. Cases involving the constitutional validity of a law of the Union or of any unit have already been dealt with; they will all necessarily fall within the Supreme Court's jurisdiction.

10. It will also, of course, be open to any Indian State unit to confer by special agreement additional jurisdiction upon the Supreme Court in respect of such matters as may be specified therein.

II. Advisory Jurisdiction of the Court

11. There has been considerable difference of opinion amongst jurists and political thinkers as to the expediency of placing on the

Supreme Court an obligation to advise the Head of the State on difficult questions of law. In spite of arguments to the contrary, it was considered expedient to confer advisory jurisdiction upon the Federal Court under the existing Constitution by section 213 of the Act. Having given our best consideration to the arguments *pros* and *cons,* we feel that it will be on the whole better to continue this jurisdiction even under the new Constitution. It may be assumed that such jurisdiction is scarcely likely to be unnecessarily invoked, and if, as we propose, the Court is to have a strength of ten or eleven judges, a pronouncement by a full court may well be regarded as authoritative advice. This can be ensured by requiring that references to the Supreme Court for advice shall be dealt with by a full court.

III. Ancillary Powers of the Court

12. Power should be conferred upon the Supreme Court as under section 214 of the Act of 1935 to make rules of procedure to regulate its work and provisions similar to those contained in Order XLV of the Civil Procedure Code should be made available so as to facilitate the preparation of the record in appeals to the Supreme Court as well as the execution of its decrees. It does not seem to us necessary to continue the restriction now placed on the Federal Court by section 209 of the Act of 1935. If the Supreme Court takes the place of the Privy Council, it may well be permitted to pronounce final judgments and final decrees in cases where this is possible or to remit the matter for further inquiry to the Courts from which the appeal has been preferred where such further inquiry is considered necessary. Provision must also be made on the lines of section 210 of the Act of 1935 giving certain inherent powers to the Supreme Court.

IV. Constitution and Strength of the Court

13. We think that the Supreme Court will require at least two Division Benches and as we think that each Division Bench should consist of five judges, the Court will require ten judges in addition to the Chief Justice so as to provide for possible absences or other unforeseen circumstances. Moreover, one of the judges may be required to deal with miscellaneous matters incidental to appellate jurisdiction (including revisional and referential jurisdictions).

V. Qualifications and Mode of Appointment of Judges

14. The qualifications of the Judges of the Supreme Court may be laid down on terms very similar to those in the Act of 1935 as regards the judges of the Federal Court, the possibility being borne in mind (as in the Act of 1935) that Judges of the superior courts even from the States which may join the Union may be found fit to occupy a seat in the Supreme Court. We do not think that it will be expedient to leave the power of appointing judges of the Supreme Court to the unfettered discretion of the President of the Union. We recommend that either of the following methods may be adopted. One method is that the President should, in consultation with the Chief Justice of the Supreme Court (so far as the appointment of *puisne* judges is concerned), nominate a person whom he considers fit to be appointed to the Supreme Court and the nomination should be confirmed by a majority of atleast 7 out of a panel of 11 composed of some of the Chief Justices of the High Courts of the constituent units, some members of both the Houses of the Central Legislature and some of the law officers of the Union. The other method is that the panel of 11 should recommend three names out of which the President, in consultation with the Chief Justice, may select a judge for the appointment. The same procedure should be followed for the appointment of the Chief Justice, except, of course, that in this case there will be no consultation with the Chief Justice. To ensure that the panel will be both independent and command confidence, the panel should not be an *ad hoc* body but must be one appointed for a term of years.

VI. Tenure of Office and Conditions of Service of Judges

15. The tenure of office of the judges of the Supreme Court will be the same as that of Federal Court judges under the present constitution Act and their age of retirement also may be the same (65). Their salary and pensions may be provided for by statutory rules. It is undesirable to have temporary judges in the highest court in the land. Instead of having temporary judges, the system of having some *ad hoc* judges out of a panel of Chief Justices or judges of the High Courts may be adopted. In this connection we invite attention to the Canadian practice as embodied in section 30 of the Canadian Supreme Act. The section runs as follows:

"30. Appointment of *ad hoc* judge: If at any time there should not be a quorum of the judges of the Supreme Court available to hold or continue any session of the Court, wing to a vacancy or vacancies, or to the absence through illness or on leave or in the discharge of other duties assigned by statute or order in council, or to the disqualification of a judgc or judges, the Chief Justice or, in his absence, the senior *puisne* judge may in writing request the attendance at the sittings of the Court, as an *ad hoc* judge, for such period as may be necessary, of a judge of the Exchequer Court, or, should the judges of the said Court be absent from Ottawa or for any reason unable to sit, of a judge of a provincial superior court to be designated in writing by the Chief Justice or in his absence by any acting Chief Justice or the senior *puisne* judge of such provincial court upon such request being made to him in writing."

4. *Duties:* It shall be the duty of the judge whose attendance has been so requested or who has been so designated in priority to other duties of his office, to attend the sittings of the Supreme Court at the time and for the period for which his attendance shall be required, and while so attending he shall possess the powers and privileges and shall discharge the duties of a *puisne* judge of the Supreme Court.

16. Not all the recommendations that we have made need find a place in the Constitution Act. The main features may be embodied in the Constitution Act and detailed provisions in a separate Judiciary Act to be passed by the Union Legislature. The form of procedure in the Supreme Court *e.g.*, for the enforcement of fundamental rights may also be provided for in the Judiciary Act. We may point out that the prerogative writs of *mandamus*, prohibition and *certiorari* have been abolished in England by a statute of 1938. Corresponding orders have been substituted and the Supreme Court of judicature has been empowered to make rules of court prescribing the procedure in cases where such orders are sought.

17. We understand our terms of reference to relate only to the constitution and powers of the Supreme Court. We have, therefore, said nothing about the High Courts of the Units, although we have had to refer to them incidentally in some of out suggestions relating to the Supreme Court.

CHAPTER IV

DRAFT CONSTITUTION PREPARED BY THE CONSTITUTION DRAFTING COMMITTEE IN FEBRUARY, 1948

Members of the Constitution Drafting Committee

1. B.R. Ambedkar
2. Alladi Krishnaswami Ayyar
3. N. Gopalaswami Ayyangar
4. K.M. Munshi
5. Mohammad Saadulla
6. D.P. Khaittan
7. N. Madhava Rao (nominated in place of B.L. Mitter on December 5, 1947)

THE FEDERAL JUDICATURE

103. (1) There shall be a Supreme Court of India consisting of a Chief Justice of India and such number of other judges not being less than seven as Parliament may by law prescribe.

(2) Every Judge of the Supreme Court shall be appointed by the President by warrant under his hand and seal after consultation with such of the Judges of the Supreme Court and of the High Courts in the States as may be necessary for the purpose and shall hold office until he attains the age of sixty-five years.

Provided that in the case of appointment of a judge, other than the Chief Justice, the Chief Justice of India shall always be consulted:

Provided further that—

(a) a Judge may, by writing under his hand addressed to the President, resign his office;

(b) a judge may be removed from his office, in the manner provided in clause (4).

(3) A person shall not be qualified for appointment as a Judge of the Supreme Court unless he is a citizen of India and—

(a) has been for a least five years a judge of a High Court or of two or more such courts in succession; or

(b) has been for at least ten years an advocate of a High Court or of two or more such courts in succession.

Explanation:—In computing for the purpose of this clause the period during which a person has been an advocate, any period during which a person held judicial office after he became an advocate, shall be included.

(4) A judge of the Supreme Court shall not be removed from his office except by an order of the President passed after an address supported by not less than two-thirds of the members present and voting has been presented to the President by both Houses of Parliament in the same session for such removal on the ground of proved misbehaviour or incapacity.

(5) Parliament may by law regulate the procedure for the presentation of an address and for the investigation and proof of the misbehaviour or incapacity of a judge under the last preceding clause.

(6) Every person appointed to be a judge of the Supreme Court shall, before he enters upon his office, make and subscribe before the President or some person appointed in that behalf by him a declaration according to the form set out for the purpose in the Third Schedule.

(7) No person who has held office as a judge of the Supreme Court shall plead or act in any court or before any authority within the territory of India.

104. The judges of the Supreme Court shall be entitled to such salaries and allowances, and to such rights in respect of leave and pensions, as may from time-to-time be fixed by or under law made by Parliament, and until they are so fixed shall be entitled to such salaries, allowances and rights in respect of leave of absence or pension as are specified in the Second Schedule:

Provided that neither the salary of a judge nor his rights in respect of leave of absence or pension shall be varied to his disadvantage after his appointment.

105. When the office of Chief Justice of India is vacant or when the Chief Justice is, by reason of absence or otherwise, unable to perform the duties of his office, the duties of the office shall be performed by such one of the other judges of the Court as the President may appoint for the purpose.

106. (1) If any time due to lack of a quorum of the judges of the Supreme Court available to hold or continue any session of the Court, the Chief Justice may after consultation with the Chief Justice of the High Court concerned, request in writing the attendance at the sittings of the Court, as an *ad hoc* judge, for such period as may be necessary, of a Judge of a High Court to be nominated by the Chief Justice of India.

(2) It shall be the duty of the judge, who has been so nominated, in priority to other duties of his office, to attend the sittings of the Supreme Court at the time and for the period for which his attendance is required, and while so attending he shall have all the jurisdiction, powers and privileges, and shall discharge the duties, of a judge of the Supreme Court.

107. Notwithstanding anything contained in this Chapter, the Chief Justice of India may at any time, subject to the provisions of this article, request any person who has held the office of a judge of the Supreme Court or of the Federal Court to sit and act as a judge of the Supreme Court, and every such person so requested shall, while so sitting and acting, have all the jurisdiction, powers and privileges of, but shall not otherwise be deemed to be, a judge of that court:

Provided that nothing in this article to sit and act as a judge of that Court unless he consents so to do.

108. The Supreme Court shall be a Court of record and shall sit in Delhi and at such other place or places, if any, as the Chief Justice may, with the approval of the President, from time to time, appoint.

109. Subject to the provisions of this Constitution, the Supreme Court shall, to the exclusion of any other court, have original jurisdiction in any dispute—

(a) between the Government of India and one or more States, or

(b) between the Government of India and any State or States on one side and one or more other States on the other, or

(c) between two or more States.

If insofar as the dispute involves any question (whether of law or fact) on which the existence or existent of a legal right depends:

Provided that the said jurisdiction shall not extend to—

(i) a dispute to which a State for the time being specified in Part III of the First Schedule is a party, if the dispute arises out of any provision of a treaty, agreement, engagement, sanad or other similar instrument which was entered into or executed before the date of commencement of this Constitution and has, or has been, continued in operation after that date;

(ii) a dispute to which any State is a party if the dispute arises out of any provision of a treaty, agreement, engagement, sanad or other similar instrument which provides that the said jurisdiction shall not extend to such a dispute.

110. (1) An appeal shall lie to the Supreme Court from any judgment, decree or final order of a High Court in a State, whether in a civil, criminal or other proceeding, if the High Court certifies that the case involves a substantial question of law as to the interpretation of this Constitution.

(2) Where the High Court has refused to give such a certificate, the Supreme Court may, if it is satisfied that the case involves a substantial question of law as to the interpretation of this Constitution, grant special leave to appeal from such judgment, decree or final order.

(3) Where such a certificate is given, or such leave is granted, any party in the case may appeal to the Supreme Court not only on the ground that any such question as aforesaid has been wrongly decided, but also on any other ground.

Explanation.—For the purpose of this article, the expression "final order" includes an order deciding an issue which, if decided in favour of the appellant, would be sufficient for the final disposal of the case.

111. (1) An appeal shall lie to the Supreme Court from a judgment, decree or final order in a civil proceeding of a High Court in the territory of India except the State for the time being specified in Part III of the First Schedule, if the High Court certifies—

(a) that the amount or value of the subject-matter of the dispute in the court of first instance and still in dispute on appeal was and is not less than twenty thousand rupees; or

(b) that the judgment, decree or final order involves directly or indirectly some claim or question respecting property of the like amount or value; or

(c) that the case is a fit one for appeal to the Supreme Court;

And, where the judgment, decree or final order appealed from affirms the decision of the Court immediately below, in any case other than one referred to in clause (c), if the High Court further certifies that the appeal involves some substantial question of law.

(2) Notwithstanding anything contained in article 110 of this Constitution, any party appealing to the Supreme Court under clause (1) of this article may urge as one of the grounds in such appeal that the case involves a substantial question of law as to the interpretation of this Constitution which has been wrongly decided.

112. The Supreme Court may, in its discretion, grant special leave to appeal from any judgment, decree or final order in any cause or matter, passed or made by any Court or Tribunal in the territory of India except the States for the time being specified in Part III of the First Schedule, in cases where the provisions of article 110 or article 111 of this Constitution do not apply.

113. (1) If in the course of any civil, criminal or other proceeding in a High Court in any State for the time being specified in Part III of the First Schedule, any question as to the applicability or interpretation of any law of Parliament or of the Legislature of any State other than such State, which is material for the determination of any issue in such preceding, arises, the High Court may, either of its own motion or on the application of any of the parties, draw up a statement of the case with particular reference to such question with its own opinion thereon and refer such question to the Supreme Court for opinion. The Supreme Court may, where any such High Court refuses to state a case under clause (1) of the article, require a case to be so stated.

(2) When a case is so stated either under clause (1) or under clause (2) of this article, the High Court shall stay all proceedings until the opinion of the Supreme Court is received.

(3) The Supreme Court shall, after giving the parties an opportunity of being heard, decide the question so referred, and shall cause a copy of its opinion to be transmitted to the High Court and such High Court shall on receipt thereof proceed to dispose of the case in conformity with the opinion of the Supreme Court.

(4) The Supreme Court may at any stage return any case stated under this article in order that further facts may be stated therein.

114. (1) The Supreme Court shall have such further jurisdiction and powers with respect to any of the matters in the Union List as Parliament may by law confer.

(2) The Supreme Court shall have such further jurisdiction and powers with respect to any matter as the Government of India and any State may by special agreement confer, if Parliament by law provides for the exercise of such jurisdiction and powers by the Supreme Court.

115. Parliament may, by law, confer on the Supreme Court power to issue directions, or orders in the nature of the writs of *habeas corpus, mandamus,* prohibition, *quo warranto* and *certiorari,* or any of them, for any purposes other than those mentioned in clause (2) of article 25 (which relates to the enforcement of fundamental rights) of this Constitution.

116. Parliament may by law make provision for conferring upon the Supreme Court such supplemental powers not inconsistent with any of the provisions of this Constitution as may appear to be necessary or desirable for the purpose of enabling the Court more effectively to exercise the jurisdiction conferred upon it by or under this Constitution.

117. The law declared by the Supreme Court shall be binding on all Courts within the territory of India.

118. (1) The Supreme Court in the exercise of its jurisdiction may pass such decree or make such order as is necessary for doing complete justice in any cause or matter pending before it, and any decree so passed or order so made shall be enforceable

throughout the territory of India in such manner as may be prescribed by or under any law made by Parliament.

(2) Subject to the provisions of any law made in this behalf by Parliament the Supreme Court shall, as respects the whole of the territory of India, have all and every power to make any order for the purpose of securing the attendance of any person, the discovery or production of any documents, or the investigation or punishment of any contempt of itself.

119. (1) If at any time it appears to the President that a question of law or fact has arisen, or is likely to arise, which is of such a nature and such public importance that it is expedient to obtain the opinion of the Supreme Court upon it, he may refer the question to that court for consideration and the court may, after such hearing as it thinks fit, report to the President its opinion.

(2) The President may, notwithstanding anything contained in clause (i) of the proviso to article 109 of this Constitution, refer a dispute of the kind mentioned in the said clause to the Supreme Court for decision, and the Supreme Court shall thereupon, after giving the parties an opportunity of being heard, decide the same and report the fact to the President.

120. All authorities, civil and judicial, in the territory of India shall act in aid of the Supreme Court.

121. (1) Subject to the provisions of any law made by Parliament, the Supreme Court may from time to time, with the approval of the President, make rules for regulating generally the practice and procedure of the Court including—

(a) rules as to the persons practicing before the Court,

(b) rules as to the procedure for hearing appeals and other matters including the time within which appeals to the Court are to be entered and the time to be allowed to advocates appearing before the Court to make their submissions in respect thereof.

(c) rules as to the cost of and incidental to any proceedings in the Court and as to the fees to be charged in respect of proceedings therein.

(d) rules as to the granting of bail.

(e) rules as to stay of proceedings, and

(f) rules providing for the summary determination of any appeal which appears to the Court to be frivolous or vexatious or brought for the purpose of delay.

(2) The minimum number of judges who are to sit for the purpose of deciding any case involving a substantial question of law as to the interpretation of this Constitution or for the purpose of hearing any reference under article 119 of this Constitution shall be five:

Provided that it shall be open to every judge to sit for the said purposes unless owing to illness, personal interest or other sufficient cause he is unable to do so.

(3) No opinion for the purpose of any report under article 119 of this Constitution and no judgment shall be delivered by the Supreme Court save in open court.

(4) No such report shall be made and no judgment shall be delivered by the Supreme Court save with the concurrence of a majority of the judges present at the hearing of the case, but nothing in this clause shall be deemed to prevent a judge who does not concur from delivering a dissenting opinion or judgment.

122. (1) The salaries, allowances and pensions payable to or in respect of the officers and servants of the Supreme Court shall be fixed by the Chief Justice of India in consultation with the President.

(2) The administrative expenses of the Supreme Court, including all salaries, allowances and pensions payable to or in respect of the officers and servants of the court, shall be charged upon the revenues of India, and any fees or other moneys taken by the Court shall form part of those revenues.

123. (1) References in articles 103 and 106 of this Chapter to a High Court in, or exercising jurisdiction in, a State for the time being specified in Part III of the First Schedule shall be construed as references to any court which the President may, upon being satisfied after consultation with the Supreme Court and the Ruler of the State that such court is a court comparable to any of the High Courts in the States for the time being specified in Part I of that Schedule, declare to be a High Court for the purposes of those articles.

(2) References in articles 110 and 113 of this Chapter to a High Court in a State for the time being specified in Part III of the First Schedule shall be construed as references to the court of final jurisdiction in the State with regard to the proceeding in respect of which an appeal or reference is provided for in those articles.

CHAPTER V

THE QUESTIONNAIRE ISSUED BY THE CONSTITUTIONAL ADVISER SHRI B.N. RAU

Regarding Judiciary:

To examine the formation of Supreme Court, it is necessary to refer to "The Questionnaire Issued by the Constitutional Adviser, Government of India". The questionnaire issued by the Constitutional Adviser, Shri B.N. Rau to the members of the Union Constitutional Committee and the Provincial Constitution Committee was a colossal document and the same also included the final shape of the Judiciary, which has to be reflected in the Constitution of India, which was before Constitutional Committee.

The Constitutional Adviser referred to the power of Federal Courts in USA, Australia and Canada.

A. U.S.A.—Under the constitution the judicial power of the United States is vested in a Supreme Court, and in such inferior courts as the Congress may from time to time ordain and establish. There are, at present, two sets of inferior Federal Courts, namely, the Federal District Courts and the Circuit Courts of Appeal. The country is divided into 83 districts, each State constituting at least one district. From the Federal Courts of these districts there is an appeal to Circuit Courts, which are ten in number. There are also two special Courts, namely the Court of Claims and the Court of Customs Appeals. In certain cases, however, the State courts may be, and are, permitted, in the exercise of the jurisdiction vested in them by the constitution or laws of their respective States, to deal with causes which are within the federal judicial power. But their jurisdiction in such cases may be qualified by the right of the defendant to have the cause removed before trial into a Federal Court, or after trial the case may be taken by appeal to the Federal Supreme Court.

B. AUSTRALIA.—The Judicial power of the Commonwealth is vested in a Federal Supreme Court, called the High Court of Australia, and "in such other federal courts as the Parliament creates, and in such other courts as it invests with federal jurisdiction". The Parliament is also empowered, to make laws investing any court of a State with federal jurisdiction. Thus the Constitution has left to the discretion of the Parliament the determination of the degree to which the agency of the State courts is to be utilized for the administration of federal laws. Under the Judiciary Act of 1903, as amended from time to time, the several courts of the States are vested with federal jurisdiction in matters not within the exclusive jurisdiction of the High Court, and there is a right of appeal from these courts to the High Court.

C. CANADA.—Under the Constitution the Canadian Parliament is empowered to establish a General Court of Appeal for Canada and other Courts for the better administration of the laws of Canada. In the exercise of these powers, the Canadian Parliament has set up a Supreme Court of Appeal and an Exchequer Court. In other respects, the administration of justice, including the Constitution, maintenance and organization of civil and criminal courts and civil procedure, is a provincial subject while criminal law and procedure are assigned to the Federation. It may be noted that the Constitution vests the Governor-General with power to appoint the judges of the superior, district, and county courts of each province, subject to certain exceptions.

PART IV

FORMATION OF SUPREME COURT, 1ST JUDGES, 1ST ATTORNEY-GENERAL AND 1ST MAJOR JUDGMENTS

OPENING OF THE SUPREME COURT OF INDIA ON 28TH JANUARY, 1950 AND INAUGURAL ADDRESSES BY SHRI MOTILAL C. SETALVAD, ATTORNEY-GENERAL

The Supreme Court of India came into existence on 26th January, 1950. The inaugural sitting of the Supreme Court of India on 28th January, 1950, was a truly memorable function. In addition to the Presiding Judges, there were present in the Court Chamber the Chief Justices of Allahabad, Assam, Bombay, Hyderabad, Madhya Bharat, Madras, Mysore, Nagpur, Orissa, PEPSU, Punjab, and Travancore-Cochin. There were also present the Advocates-General of Allahabad, Bombay, Bihar, East Punjab, Madhya Bharat, Madras, Mysore, Orissa and the U.P. In addition, the Prime Minister of India, the Deputy Prime Minister and other Ministers, Ambassadors, Ministers and diplomatic representatives of foreign States and several other dignitaries were also present.

The proceedings opened with a speech by the Attorney-General. He accorded the supreme Tribunal of the Indian Union a cordial welcome not only on behalf of the Advocates-General of the States and distinguished members of the Bar present, but on behalf of the Bar and the legal profession throughout the country. He referred to the inauguration of the Federal Court of India twelve years before the inauguration of the Supreme Court, and pointed out how during the short period of its existence, the Federal Court had within its limited sphere, laid truly and strong foundations of constitutional law and practice in the country. He further said that it built up a great tradition, and, not infrequently, in the turbulent years which followed the War, it stood between the arbitrary action of the Executive and the people, "endeavouring to safeguarding the liberty of the subject". He referred to the areas, extent and nature of the jurisdiction of the Supreme Court and the great responsibility which the Constitution had placed on the Court. He said as follows:—

> "The writ of this Court will run over territory extending to over two million square miles inhabited by a population of about 330 million. It can truly be said that the jurisdiction and powers of this Court, in their nature and extent, are wider than those exercised by the highest court of any country in the Commonwealth or by the Supreme Court of the United States".

He then reminded the court that the foremost task will be to interpret the Constitution which is but a means of ordering the life of a progressive people. The Federal Court has already laid down that a Constitution is to be interpreted in no narrow spirit. For, in the words of Justice Holmes of the United States, "The provisions of the Constitution are no mathematical formulae having their essence in the form; they are organic living institutions. Their significance is vital, not formal, it is to be gathered not simply by taking the words and a dictionary but by considering their origin and the line of their growth. The essence of a federation is the division of power between two governments in the same territory. In the large area of inter-section of Union and State authority, the Court will be called upon to mark the boundaries between State and Union action and to adjust the relationship of the Union to the States. The vital share of the United States in the interplay of the country's political and economic force is well-known. So great has been its contribution in American legal and political thought that today, in the words of an American writer, an "attitude of adoration and almost working of the Court" has become general and customary among large group of people. Justices of the Court are not architects of policy. They can nullify the policy of others," says a great jurist. This power of negation exercised with "judicial statesmanship" has earned the Supreme Court a high place in the hearts of a large number of Americans.

Our Constitution is, in many respects, essentially different. The division of powers between the Union and the States has been carefully planned. Yet, many vital domestic issues are bound to arise in variety of forms before the Court, and its decisions are sure to exercise a far-reaching influence on these issues.

He also referred to the role of the Supreme Court as under:—

> "The role which the Court will be called upon to play in mediating between the individual and the Government. The detailed enumeration of fundamental rights in the Constitution and the provisions which enable them to be reasonably restricted will need wise and discriminating decisions. On the Court will fall the delicate and difficult task of ensuring to the citizen the enjoyment of his guaranteed rights consistently with the rights of the society and the State".

He called attention to the great role performed by the Privy Council which has so well and so ably functioned as the highest Court of Appeal for about a hundred years. The great Judges who have from time to time presided over its deliberations have left a deep and ineffaceable impression on the law of this country. Our tie with the Judicial Committee of the Privy Council has now snapped. But the law laid down in their judgments will doubtless continue to mould and influence the decisions of this Court. This is inevitable, because the roots of our statute law and legal forms lie deeply enmeshed in the jurisprudence of England, and the decisions of the English Courts.

In concluding his speech, he said:—

> "We at the Bar have confidence that the Supreme Court of India, which is being inaugurated today, will, in course of time, attain the same judicial eminence, and that memorable and epoch-making judgments will illumine its records. The task before us all is the building of a nation alive to its national and international duties, consisting of a strong Central Authority and federated units each possessed of ample power for the diverse uses of a progressive people. In the attainment of this noble end, we hope and trust that this Court will play a great and singular role and establish itself in the consciousness of the Indian people. "Like all

human institutions, the Supreme Court,' we hope, will earn reverence through truth".

SHRI HON'BLE SIR HARILAL JEKISUNDAS KANIA, CHIEF JUSTICE OF INDIA

In a democratic country, the people make the law through their legislature. It is not the function of the Court to supervise or correct the laws passed by the legislature as an overriding authority. It is its function and duty to point out, when examining the acts of individuals or of the executive authority purporting to be done under some Act of the legislature, the lacunae or loopholes only with the object that, if so desired, the legislative authority may put matters right. As it is often stated, in cases of hardship, the Court tries its best to do justice between the parties; but, if a clear provision of law exists, it has to administer the law, and not make one. The Court is thus working always in co-operation with the legislature and at no time its work can be considered obstructive or its attitude antagonistic.

Referring to the role of the Court in interpreting the Constitution, he said:—

"The duty of interpreting that Constitution with an enlightened liberality falls on the Supreme Court. The Supreme Court will declare and interpret the law of the land, and, with the high traditions behind the Judiciary of this country, we are convinced that the work will be done in no spirit of formal or barren legalism. It will be our endeavour to interpret the Constitution, not as a rigid body, but, as a living organism, having within itself the force and power of self-government. We trust, that, in doing so, we shall allow the constitutional usages and conventions recognized in all civilized independent countries to be respected. The Supreme Court, however, under the colour of interpretation, cannot alter or amend the law. But, within the limits prescribed, we are quite sure that the Supreme Court will be able to make a substantial contribution towards the formation of India into a great unit retaining its own civilization, traditions and customs. With the establishment of the Supreme Court of India, we shall develop our own jurisprudence based on our historical background and we trust that that will be an important and useful contribution to the creation of International Law. The Federal Court, as interpreting the Constitution of the country, had earned the confidence of the country. In endowing the Supreme Court of India with very wide powers, the Constituent Assembly- the Assembly representing the voice of the people through its elected representatives- has shown complete confidence in the Court as the final body for dispensing justice between individuals and also between States and States, and the States and the Centre. We hope to deserve that confidence. We trust that the people of India will also maintain the independence, honour and dignity of the Supreme Court".

Inviting the co-operation of the Bar in the Court's lofty endeavour he said:

"The Indian Bar has maintained the high tradition of the profession. Different conditions in different provinces have so far prevented the creation of one Bar with one good reliable standards of advocacy, knowledge and etiquette. With the inauguration of the Independent Republic of India and the States Union Courts attaining the status of the States High Courts, one can look forward in time to the existence of one Bar for India, with a very high standard of efficiency to assist the Courts in the administration of justice".

Finally the learned Chief Justice envisaged the Court playing the independent and impartial role in the life of the country;

The Supreme Court, an all-India Court will stand firm and aloof from party politics and political theories. It is unconcerned with the changes in the Government. The Court stands to administer the law for the time being in force, has goodwill and sympathy for all, but is allied to none. Occupying that position, we hope and trust it will play a great part in the building-up of the nation, and in stabilizing the roots of civilization which have twice been threatened and shaken by two world wars, and maintain the fundamental principles of justice which are the emblem of God.

The Chief Justice of India read, before he concluded his speech, a message received from the Lord Chancellor of England on the occasion. In the course of the message, the Lord Chancellor said:—

"It is satisfactory to think that, notwithstanding all the difficulties of the day, we are all determined to maintain and strengthen the rule of law, and I feel quite confident that the

Supreme Court of India will prove an effective instrumental for this end.

I like to think that you share with us common traditions and I feel sure that we shall each gain strength and wisdom from the development of each other's jurisprudence".

The sitting terminated with a formal request by the Attorney-General that all advocates on the record of the Federal Court be brought on record on the rolls of the Supreme Court, and the Chief Justice pointing out that this had been provided for under the rules made by the Court.

(Taken from Chapter Six of the Book My Life Law and other Things by Shri Motilal C. Setalvad)

PART V

IMPORTANT JUDGMENTS DELIVERED BY THE CONSTITUTION BENCH OF SUPREME COURT

Soon after the inauguration of the Hon'ble Supreme Court, the Court was called upon to examine one of the most important articles in the Constitution article 21, which dealt with personal liberty, the question having arisen on a challenge to the validity of the Preventive Detention Act which the learned Attorney-General had supported in Parliament. It was also probably the first petition heard by the Court under article 32 of the Constitution which confers on the citizen a right to move the Supreme Court for relief in respect of a fundamental right and is itself made a guaranteed right.

Gopalan's case[1], which is said to have made legal history, arose out of a petition for a writ of *habeas corpus* against the detention of Gopalan, a communist, in the Madras Jail. He had been from time to time under detention since December, 1947, though finally acquitted of the charges in respect of which he had been sentenced to imprisonment by the courts. While still under detention under the orders of the State Government, on the 1st March, 1950, Gopalan was served with an order made under the Preventive Detention Act. The Chief Justice in his judgment described the petition as "the first case in which the different articles of the Constitution of India contained in the Chapter on Fundamental Rights have come for discussion before us." The petitioner was represented by M.L. Nambiar who in presenting his first argument in the Supreme Court showed himself to be an able constitutional lawyer.

1. *A.K. Gopalan* v. *The State of Madras*, 1950 SCR 88.

It was not surprising that the hearing of the petition took several days as far-reaching and complex questions were raised by the petitioner's counsel. Nambiar, in his thorough and exhaustive manner, put forward every conceivable argument in support of the petition, and the Chief Justice rightly acknowledged in the judgment the Court's indebtedness to him for his assistance in interpreting the true meaning of the relevant clauses of the Constitution.

Of the large number of questions raised before the Court, two questions were basic. Did article 19(1)(d) of the Constitution, which conferred on all citizens "the right to move freely throughout the territory of India", confer a right to personal liberty which was infringed by the law of preventive detention which kept a person under detention in a jail? What was the true interpretation of article 21, which provided that "no person shall be deprived of his life or personal liberty except according to procedure established by law?".

The contention of the applicant was that article 19(1) and article 21 were to be read together and that the right to movement throughout the territory of India conferred by Article 19(1)(d) of the Constitution was merely an amplification of the right to personal liberty which had been embodied in article 21 of the Constitution. The majority of the Court rejected this contention, basing itself upon the view that article 19(1), which was only available to citizens dealt only with certain aspects of liberty which could be enjoyed only if the citizen was free. The right of locomotion all over the country conferred by article 19(1)(d) could therefore apply only to a person who was free. It could not be availed of by a person who had been sentenced to imprisonment under law or to a person who had been lawfully detained under a law of preventive detention.

The courts are not at liberty to declare an Act void because in their opinion it is opposed to a spirit supposed to pervade the Constitution but not expressed in words. Where the fundamental law has not limited, either in terms or by necessary implication, the general powers conferred upon the Legislature we cannot declare a limitation under the notion of having discovered something in the spirit of the Constitution which is not even mentioned in the instrument. It is difficult upon any general principles to limit the *omnipotence* of the sovereign legislative power by judicial interposition, except so far as the express words of a written Constitution give that authority. It is also stated, if the words be positive and without ambiguity, there is no authority for a Court to vacate or repeal a Statute on that ground alone.

The case was heard by a Constitution Bench consisting of Shri Harilal Kania, Chief Justice, Saiyid Fazl Ali, Patanjali Sastri, Mehr Chand Mahajan, Mukherjea and S.R. Das, JJ. The majority judgment was delivered by Kania, Chief Justice, Patanjali Sastri, Mukherjea and Das. JJ.

"*Inter-alia* it was held that the Preventive Detention Act, 1950, with the exception of section 14 thereof did not contravene any of the Articles of the Constitution and even though section 14 was *ultra vires* inasmuch as it contravened the provisions of article 22(5) of the Constitution, as this section was severable from the remaining sections of the Act, the invalidity of section 14 did not affect the validity of the Act as a whole, and the detention of the petitioner was not illegal.

Fazl Ali and Mahajan, JJ.—Section 12 of the Act was also *ultra vires,* and since it contravened the very provision in the Constitution under which the Parliament derived its competence to enact the law, the detention was illegal.

Held, by the Full Court (Kania, CJ., Fazl Ali, Patanjali Shastri, Mahajan, Mukherjea and Das, JJ.)—Section 14 of the Preventive Detention Act, 1950, contravenes the provisions of article 22(5) of the Constitution insofar as it prohibits a person detained form disclosing to the Court the grounds on which a detention order has been made or the representation made by him against the order of detention, and is to that extent *ultra vires* and void."

In the concluding portion of this judgment Mr. Justice Fazl Ali held as under:—

> "That a person should be deprived of his personal liberty without a trial is a serious matter, but the needs of society may demand it and the individual may often have to yield to those needs. Still the balance between the maintenance of individual rights and public good can be struck only if the person who is deprived of his liberty is allowed a fair chance to establish his innocence, and I do not see

how the establishment of an appropriate machinery giving him such a chance can be an impediment to good and just government."

"The learned Attorney-General's observations however on the judgment are important and far-reaching. It is clear that the time is not far distant when the Supreme Court will have to modify the view taken by it of article 21 in its earliest decision dealing with fundamental rights".

Another notable application under Article 32 of the Constitution which the Court had to deal with soon after its inauguration was one which raised for the first time before the Court the true meaning of article 14 of the Constitution. This was filed by Chiranjitlal, a shareholder of the Sholapur Spinning & Weaving Co. Ltd.[2]"

The Sholapur Mills had closed down and the Governor-General of India issued an Ordinance in January, 1950, marking special provisions for the proper management and administration of the affairs of the Mills company. The Preamble to the Ordinance recited that, on account of mismanagement and neglect, a situation had arisen in the affairs of the company which had prejudicially affected the production of an essential commodity and had caused serious unemployment amongst a certain section of the community. Later, the Ordinance was repealed and an Act was passed by Parliament, re-enacting almost in identical terms all the provisions of the Ordinance.

By the Act, power was taken by the Central Government to appoint directors of the company for the purpose of taking over its management and administration, one of such directors being appointed the chairman. The directors of the company holding office immediately before the issue of the Ordinance were removed.

The directors appointed by the Government were given wide powers, including the power (with the previous sanction of the Central Government) to vary or cancel any contract or agreement entered into between the company and any other persons, if they were satisfied that such contract or agreement was detrimental to the interests of the company. It was further

---

2. *Chiranjitlal Chowdhuri* v. *Union of India,* 1950 SCR 869.

provided that, so long as the management by the statutory directors continued, the share-holders were to be precluded from nominating or appointing any persons to be directors of the company.

The validity of the Ordinance and the act was attacked on various grounds such as the contravention of articles 14, 19(1)(f) and article 31(2) of the Constitution. By a majority, the Court negatived the contentions based on article 19(1)(f) and article 31(2) as it took the view that the petitioner-share-holder had no rights as such share-holder in the property of the company, and that the company itself, though a respondent, was not the petitioner. However, the importance of the case lay in the manner in which the Court dealt with the contentions based on article 14 of the Constitution. The petitioner's argument was that the Act was a piece of discriminatory legislation contravening article 14 which guaranteed to all persons equality before the law and equal protection of the laws. It was urged that the entire object of that article was to prevent any person or class of persons from being singled out as a special object of hostile legislation. It was argued that the Legislature had singled out one particular company and its share-holders for dispossessing them of the right to manage their own affairs, though the same treatment had not been meted out to other companies or shareholders in an identical situation.

When dealing with article 21 of the Constitution, the Court, with justification, had refused to apply American decisions based on the totally different language used in the American Constitution. But article 14 closely corresponded to the 14th amendment of the American Constitution, which declared that "no State shall deny to any person within its jurisdiction the equal protection of laws". The Court considered the American decisions on the subject and imported into India the doctrine of reasonable classification.

The Court boldly laid down that the legislature had a wide field of choice in determining and classifying the subject of its laws, and if the law dealt alike with all of a certain class, it was normally not open to the charge of denial of equal protection. But the classification could not be arbitrary. To be valid, it had necessarily to rest upon some real and substantial distinction bearing a reasonable and just relation to the things in respect of which the classification was made. These principles laid down by Justice Mukherjea, have stood the test of time and been uniformly applied in later cases decided by the Court.

The case was heard by a Constitution Bench consisting of Shri Harilal Kania, Chief Justice, Saiyid Fazl AN, Patanjali Sastri, Mukherjea and Das, JJ.

In the concluding portion of this judgment, Mr. Justice Das held as under:—

> "In any event, the petitioner, in my opinion may well claim to have discharged the *onus* of showing that this company and its share-holders have been singled out for discriminating treatment by showing that the act, on the face of it, has adopted a basis of classification which, by its very nature, cannot be exclusively applicable to this company and its share-holders but which may be equally applicable to other companies and their share-holders and has penalized this particular company and its share-holders, leaving out other companies and their share-holders who may be equally guilty of the alleged vice of mismanagement and neglect of the type referred to in the Preambles. In my opinion the legislation in question infringes the fundamental rights of the petitioner and offends against article 14 of our Constitution."

PART VI

SUPREME COURT OF INDIA—RETROSPECT & PROSPECT

On the 26th day of January, 1950, the people of India solemnly resolved to constitute a sovereign, democratic, republic and gave to themselves a constitution. The Constitution established a federation of the Union and States, Parliamentary institutions, a Bill of Rights in the form of a chapter on "Fundamental Rights", innovative "Directive Principles of State Policy" and a Judiciary headed by the Supreme Court of India, with High Courts for every State, empowered to interpret and give effect of the Constitution and defend the rights and liberties of all persons and citizens.

On January 28, 1950, two days after India became sovereign democratic republic, the Supreme Court had its inaugural session. The inauguration took place in the Chamber of Princes in the Parliament building, which also housed India's Parliament, consisting of the Council of States and the House of the People.

Chief Justice Harilal J. Kania observed in inaugural session that "The Supreme Court, an all India Court, will stand firm and aloof from party politics and political theories. It is unconcerned with the changes in the Government. The Court stands to administer the law for the time being in force, has goodwill and sympathy for all, but is allied to none."

The Supreme Court established by the Constitution was empowered with a jurisdiction for greater than that of any comparable court anywhere in the world. It could virtually hear, decide and pronounce on any legal matter brought before it.

SUPREME COURT ARCHITECTURE

The main block of Supreme Court building was built on triangular plot of 17 acres and the building was designed by Chief architect Ganesh Bhikaji Deolalikar who was the first Indian to head CPWD and designed Supreme Court Building in an Indo-British architectural style. He was succeeded by Shridher Krishna Joglekar. The foundation stone of the Supreme Court Building was laid by the first President of India, Dr. Rajendra Prasad on 29th October, 1954.

The broad decision taken at the highest level in 1956 was that the 'Supreme Court Building should be constructed in the **triangular plot** on Hardinge Avenue opposite Hardinge Bridge. Subsequently, the area has been rechristened and now the building is surrounded by Tilak Marg in the West, Mathura Road in the East and Bhagwan Dass Road in the South and Tilak Bridge in the North.

The design of the building itself is in the shape of a balance with a pair of Scales of Justice. This noble edifice has been conceived and planned by Engineers and Architects who were trained in their profession according to western standards. The architecture and construction of Building bear testimony of their western experience and skill of high order and they have combined with it Indian conception of justice. Traditionally justice is looked upon as a pair of scales the two pans of which have to be held evenly without allowing the beam from which they hang to incline to one side or the other. Therefore, there are two wings on the two sides. They will accommodate the offices and the records. At the end of each wing is a semi-circular structure. They represent the pans which are attached to the beam at the top. This beam will accommodate the Court rooms wherein the Hon'ble Judges will sit and dispense justice without inkling either to the right or to the left.

The Central beam from the ends of which the scales hang, comprises the Chief Justice's Court at the Centre with two Court halls on either side. The right wing of the structure consists of the Bar room, the offices of the Attorney-General and other Law officers and the library of the Court. The left wing consists of offices of the Court.

• MOTHER AND CHILD SCULPTURE

A black bronze sculpture of 210 centimeter height was installed in lawn of the Supreme Court on 20 February, 1978. It portrays **Mother India** in the form of the **figure of a lady.** The lady is sheltering the young Republic of India represented by the symbol of a child, who is upholding the laws of land symbolically shown in the form of an open book. On the book, a balance is shown, which represents dispensation of equal justice to all. The sculpture was made by the renowned artist Shri Chintamoni Kar.

• LOGO OF THE SUPREME COURT—DHARMA CHAKRA

Design of Logo is reproduced from the wheel that appears on the abacus of the **Sarnath Lion Capital of Ashoka** with 32 spokes. The inscription in Sanskrit **"yatodharmastato jayah"** means – **Truth alone I uphold.** It is also referred to – as the wheel of righteousness, encompassing truth, goodness and equity.

THE HISTORY—FEDERAL COURT

It is said that – roots of the present lay deep in the past. In order to understand the present, it may be worth taking a few steps back and looking at the times of the British.

Government of India Act, 1935 enacted on 2nd August, 1935. In Part IX namely "The Judicature" it was laid down that "There shall be a Federal Court consisting of a Chief Justice of India and such number of other Judges as His Majesty may deem necessary. It also provided that the number of *puisne* Judges shall not exceed six." It was established as a Court of Record which shall sit in Delhi.

A Federal system, in its actual operation, depends very largely upon a just and competent administration of the law as between Government themselves, as between Government and the people, and as between individual persons.

It was the first Constitutional Court and also the first all India Court of extensive jurisdiction having **Original, Appellate** and **Advisory Jurisdiction.** Law declared by the Federal Court and Privy Council had been given binding effect on all the Courts in British India. The Federal Court had its inaugural Session on December 6, 1937 in Chamber of Princess in Parliament Building,

New Delhi and sat there for 12 years until Supreme Court of India replaced it.

The first sitting of Federal Court makes an epoch in the history of India. The establishment of the Court introduced a new element in the Indian jurisprudence - one of oldest and greatest civilizations of the World. In exercise of both its original and appellate jurisdiction, the Federal Court exercised its responsibility in such a manner that the quality of judicial capacity, fairness, and dignity, based upon British tradition, has gained so high a reputation.

Appeals from the Federal Court lay to the Privy Council in London, which remained the final Arbitrator on all the matters of Indian Legal System. The Federal Court in its existence for 12 years left behind a considerable impact on Indian law. The First Chief Justice of the Federal Court was **Sir Maurice Gwyer.** During the period of its existence, the Federal Court decided 151 cases on issues of momentous importance relating to federalism, its own Advisory jurisdiction and, on matters of Preventive detention. In 1950, when the Federal Court ceased to exist, its Judges became the Judges of the Supreme Court of India, carrying out with them tradition of erudition, independence and courage for its successor Court to follow.

SUPREME COURT OF INDIA—JURISDICTION

The Supreme Court of India has the **Original, Appellate** and **Advisory Jurisdiction.** The **Original Jurisdiction** is used rarely by entertaining a Writ Petition under article 32 of the Constitution for the protection of fundamental rights. The primary task of the Supreme Court is appellate and in that capacity it serves as final Arbitrator in the construction of Constitutional Provisions, Appeals comes to the Supreme Court from various sources, *i.e.,* from High Court, Tribunals and Special Tribunals etc. The different types of **Jurisdictions** given to the Supreme Court under the Constitutional scheme are as under:-

I. ORIGINAL JURISDICTION

(a) Writ Jurisdiction

Under article 32, the Supreme Court has powers to issue directions or orders including writs in the nature of ***Habeas Corpus, Mandamus,*** **Prohibition,** ***Quo Warranto*** **and** ***Certiorari,*** whichever may be appropriate, for the enforcement of any of the fundamental rights guaranteed under the Constitution.

(b) Election Disputes Relating to President/Vice-President of India

In view of article 71, disputes relating to the election of the President or Vice-President of the Union of India may be enquired into, and decided by the Supreme Court whose decision shall be final.

(c) Original Suits

In the case of contingencies enumerated under article 131, the Supreme Court can exercise original jurisdiction to the exclusion of any other Court. Disputes between the Government of India and one or more States; or between the Government of India and any State or States on the other; or between two or more States, fall in this category.

(d) Transfer of Cases

The Supreme Court also has powers to transfer matters from one High Court to another High Court or from one Court subordinate to another Court subordinate to another High Court under section 25 of the Code of Civil Procedure, 1973. The Supreme Court can also transfer to itself any case involving same or substantially same questions of law pending before it and one or more High Courts in certain contingencies as per the provisions under article 139A.

(e) Arbitration Matters

"The Appointment of Arbitrators by the Chief Justice of India Scheme, 1996" framed under section 11(10) of the Arbitration and Conciliation Act, 1996 regulates the appointment of arbitrators under section 11(6) of the Act.

(f) Contempt Proceedings

The Supreme Court of India has all the powers to punish for contempt of itself. For this purpose, "Rules to Regulate proceedings for Contempt of the Supreme Court, 1975," have been framed in exercise of the power under section 23 of the Contempt of Courts Act, 1971, read with article 145 of the Constitution of India.

II. APPELLATE JURISDICTION

(a) General

Appellate Jurisdiction is exercised under articles 132 to 134 of the Constitution. According to article 132, an appeal shall lie to the Supreme Court from any Judgment, Decrees or Final Order of a High Court in the territory of India, whether in a civil, criminal or other proceedings, if the High Court certifies under article 134A that the case involves a substantial question of law as to the interpretation of the Constitution. An appeal shall also lie to Supreme Court from any Judgment, Decree of Final Order in civil proceedings of a High Court, if the High Court certifies under article 134A(a) that the case involves substantial question of law of general importance; and (b) that in the opinion of the High Court, the said question needs to be decided by the Supreme Court. In criminal matters, article 134 provides for appeal to Supreme Court upon the High Court issuing a certificate about fitness of the cases for such appeal, or where sentence of death is awarded by the High Court reversing an order of acquittal by trial court, or in a case tried by the High Court, awards a sentence of death.

(b) Statutory Appeals

A number of special statutes provide for appeal to Supreme Court.

(c) Special Leave Petitions

The provision most resorted to is article 136 providing for Special Leave to Appeal. In cases other than those in which leave has been granted by the High Court, leave may be granted by the Supreme Court in its discretion. The proceedings are popularly referred to as "SLP".

(d) Reference

Income Tax Appellate Tribunal, through its President, can refer to Supreme Court under section 257 of the Income Tax Act, 1961, any question of law regarding which there is conflict in the decisions of High Courts and it is expedient that a reference should be made to the Supreme Court.

III. ADVISORY JURISDICTION

(i) If at any time it appears to the President of India that a question of law or fact of such public importance has arisen (or is likely to arise) and that it is expedient to obtain the opinion, he may refer the question to the Supreme Court for consideration (article 143). The Court on receiving such a reference may, after hearing, as it thinks fit, report to the President its opinion thereon.

(ii) The reference to the Supreme Court can also be made as in:—

(a) Article 317, as regards removal of Chairman or any other Member of a Public Services Commission;

(b) Section 11 of the Competition Act, 2002 as regards removal of a Member of the Competition Commission; and

(c) Removal of Chief Information Commissioner or Information Commissioner, State Chief Information Commissioner as per sections 14 and 17 of the Right to Information Act, 2005.

IV. POWER OF REVIEW

The Supreme Court, under article 137, has the power to review any of its judgments or orders made by it. Review Petitions are disposed of by circulation as per listing procedures.

PUBLIC UTILITY FACILITIES AT SUPREME COURT

In the premises of Supreme Court, various public utility facilities have been made available for the benefit of the advocates, litigants, Officers and staff of the Registry:—

Post Office

A huge number of letters, notices, documents, parcels etc. are to be dispatched by the Registry to Advocates and various outside agencies, High Courts, various departments of Centre and State Governments and lawyers throughout the country. The Post Office facility, has been made available within the premises of the Supreme Court to facilitate the same.

Banking Services

In order to facilitate the financial transactions, a full-fledged branch of United Commercial Bank is operating in the premises of Supreme Court of India. A separate counter has been opened by the Bank to give better services to the advocates, Officers and staff of the Registry. Two ATMs are also operational within Supreme Court premises for facilitating the cash withdrawal round the clock.

Railway Reservation Counter

Advocates and litigants from all over India come to the Supreme Court for their cases. In order to facilitate the railway reservation for them and also for the Hon'ble Judges, Officers and staff of the Registry, a separate "Railway Reservation Counter" has been opened in the Supreme Court premises to provide reservation facilities.

Dispensary

In order to provide medical facilities to the Hon'ble Judges, Officers and staff of the Registry, Supreme Court Dispensary (First Aid Post) was established within the premises of the Supreme Court in the year 1989. In addition to the regular Doctors, Medical Specialists in various specialized fields also visit the Dispensary twice/thrice a week. A Pathological Laboratory and a Physiotherapy wing is also available in this Dispensary.

Canteen Facility

A separate Canteen and Cafeteria for the advocates and a Canteen run by the Supreme Court for its Officers and staff are also operational in the Supreme Court premises.

STRENGTH OF SUPREME COURT JUDGES AT DIFFERENT TIMES

The strength of Supreme Court Judges is prescribed under article 124(1) of the Constitution of India. It has been increased from time to time by way of Constitutional amendments.

The Supreme Court **started** with the strength of 7 Judges and one Chief Justice of India in the year **1950.** By **Act No. 55 of 1956,** the strength of Supreme Court Judges was increased to 10 Judges and the Chief Justice of India. In the year **1960,** the strength of Supreme Court Judges was once again increased by **Act No. 17 of 1960.** By this Act, the strength of Judges was increased to **13** Judges and the Chief Justice of India. By **Act No. 48 of 1977**, the strength of Supreme Court Judges was further increased to **17** and the Chief Justice of India. **Act No. 22 of 1986,** further increased the strength of Supreme Court Judges **from 17 to 25** and the Chief Justice of India and since **2009,** the strength was increased to **30** and the Chief Justice of India by **Act No. 11 of 2009.**

ORGANISATIONAL STRUCTURE OF S.C. REGISTRY

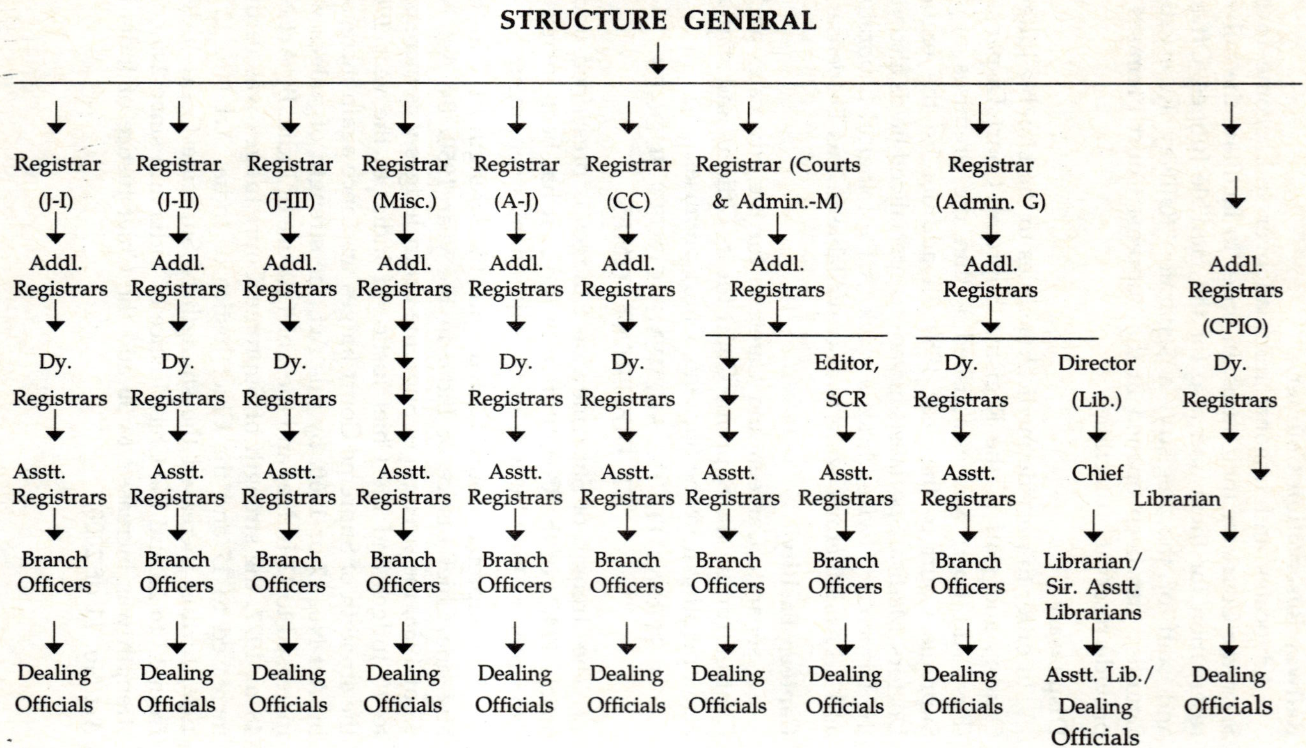

STAFF STRENGTH IN THE SUPREME COURT OF INDIA

With the increasing work load in the Registry, like the increasing strength of Judges of Supreme Court, staff strength in the Supreme Court Registry also increased substantially. There are now 2142 sanctioned posts in the Supreme Court Registry at different levels as against 71 sanctioned post in the year 1950. Out of 2142 sanctioned posts, there are 277 (11 in 1950) Gazetted posts, 1030 (21 in 1950) Non-Gazetted posts and 835 (39 in 1950) Class IV posts. Registry is headed by Secretary-General, who is assisted by the Registrar at the next hierarchy.

These statistics of Staff strength in tabular form are as under:—

S. No.	Nature of Posts	Sanctioned posts in 1950	Sanctioned posts in 2014
1.	Gazetted	11	277
2.	Non-Gazetted	21	1030
3.	Class-IV (Erstwhile)	39	835
	Total	**71**	**2142**

PART VII

EXISTING PROVISIONS IN THE CONSTITUTION OF INDIA RELATING TO THE UNION JUDICIARY

124. Establishment and Constitution of Supreme Court.—(1) There shall be a Supreme Court of India consisting of a Chief Justice of India, until Parliament by law prescribes a larger number, of not more than seven other Judges.

(2) Every Judge of the Supreme Court shall be appointed by the President by warrant under his hand and seal after consultation with such of the Judges of the Supreme Court and of the High Courts in the States, as the President may deem necessary for the purpose and shall hold office until he attains the age of sixty-five years.

Provided that in the case of appointment of a Judge other than the Chief Justice, the Chief Justice of India shall always be consulted:

Provided further that—

(a) a Judge may, by writing under his hand addressed to the President, resign his office;

(b) a Judge may be removed from his office in the manner provided in clause (4)

(2A) The age of a judge of the Supreme Court shall be determined by such authority and in such manner as Parliament may by law provide.

(4) A person shall not be qualified for appointment as a Judge of the Supreme Court unless he is a citizen of India and—

(a) has been for at least five years a Judge of a High Court or of two or more such Courts in succession; or

(b) has been for at least ten years an advocate of a High Court or of two or more such courts in succession; or

(c) is, in the opinion of the President, a distinguished jurist.

Explanation I—In this clause "High Court" means a High Court which exercises or which at any time before the commencement of this Constitution exercised, jurisdiction in any part of the territory of India.

Explanation II—In computing for the purpose of this clause the period during which a person has been an advocate, any period during which a person has held judicial office not inferior to that of a district judge after he became an advocate should be included.

(5) A Judge of the Supreme Court shall not be removed form his office except by an order of the President passed after an address by each House of Parliament supported by a majority of the total membership of that House and by a majority of not less than two-thirds of the members of the House present and voting has been presented to the President in the same session for such removal on the ground of proved misbehaviour or incapacity.

(6) Parliament may by law regulate the procedure for the presentation of an address and for the investigation and proof of the misbehaviour or incapacity of a Judge under clause (4).

(7) Every person appointed to be a Judge of the Supreme Court shall, before he enters upon his office, make and subscribed before the President, or some person appointed in that behalf by him, an oath or affirmation according to the form set out for the purpose in the Third Schedule.

No person, who has held office as a Judge of the Supreme Court shall plead or act in any Court or before any authority within the territory of India.

125. Salaries, etc., of Judges.—(1) There shall be paid to the Judges of the Supreme Court such salaries as may be determined by Parliament by law and, until provision in that behalf is so made, such salaries are specified in the Second Schedule.

(2) Every Judge shall be entitled to such privileges and allowances and to such rights in respect of leave of absence and pension as may from time to time be determined by or under law made by Parliament and, until so determined, to such privileges, allowances and rights as are specified in the Second Schedule:

Provided that neither the privileges nor the allowances of a Judge nor his rights in respect of leave of absence or pension shall be varied to his disvantage after his appointment.

126. Appointment of acting Chief Justice.—When the office of Chief Justice of India is vacant or when the Chief Justice is by, reason of absence or otherwise, unable to perform the duties of his office, the duties of the office shall be performed by such one of the other Judges of the Court as the President may appoint for the purpose.

127. Appointment of *ad hoc* Judges.—(1) If at any time there should not be a quorum of the Judges of the Supreme Court available to hold or continue any session of the Court, the Chief Justice of India may, with the previous consent of the President and after consultation with the Chief Justice of the High Court concerned, request in writing the attendance at the sittings of the Court, as an *ad hoc* Judge, for such period as may be necessary, of a Judge of a High Court duly qualified for appointment as a Judge of the Supreme Court to be designated by the Chief Justice of India.

(2) It shall be the duty of the Judge who has been so designated, in priority to other duties of his office, to attend the sittings of the Supreme Court at the time and for the period for which his attendance is required, and while so attending he shall have all the jurisdiction, powers and privileges, and shall discharge the duties, of a Judge of the Supreme Court.

128. Attendance of retired Judges at sittings of the Supreme Court.—Notwithstanding anything in this chapter, the Chief Justice of India may at any time, with the previous consent of the President, request any person who has held the office of a Judge of the Supreme Court or of the federal Court or who has held the office of a Judge of a High Court and duly qualified for appointment as a Judge of the Supreme Court to sit and act as a Judge of the Supreme Court, and every such person so requested shall, while so sitting and acting, be entitled to such allowances as the President may by order determine and have all the jurisdiction, powers and privileges of, but shall not otherwise be deemed to be, a Judge of that Court:

Provided that nothing in this article shall be deemed to require any such person as aforesaid to sit and act as a Judge of that Court unless he consents so to do.

129. Supreme Court to be a Court of record.—The Supreme Court shall be a Court of record and shall have all the powers of such a Court including the powers to punish for contempt of itself.

130. Seat of Supreme Court.—The Supreme Court shall sit in Delhi or in such other place or places, as the Chief Justice of India may, with the approval of the President, from time to time, appoint.

131. Original jurisdiction of the Supreme Court.—Subject to the provisions of this Constitution, the Supreme Court shall, to the exclusion of any other Court, have original jurisdiction in any dispute-

(a) between the Government of India and one or more States; or

(b) between the Government of India and any State or States on one side and one or more other States on the other; or

(c) between two or more States.

If and is so far as the dispute involves any question (whether or law or fact) on which the existence or extent of a legal right depends:

Provided that the said jurisdiction shall not extend to a dispute arising out of any treaty, agreement, covenant, engagement, sanad or other similar instrument which, having been entered into or executed before the commencement of this Constitution, continues in operation after such commencement, or which provides that the said jurisdiction shall not extend to such a dispute.

132. Appellate jurisdiction of Supreme Court in Appeals from High Courts in certain cases.—(1) An appeal shall lie to the Supreme Court from any judgment, decree or final order of a High Court in the territory of India, whether in a civil, criminal or other proceeding, (if the High Court certifies under article 134A) that the case involves a substantial question of law as to the interpretation of this Constitution.

(2) Where such a certificate is given any party in the case may appeal to the Supreme Court on the ground that any such question as aforesaid has been wrongly decided.

Explanation—for the purposes of this article, the expression "final order" includes an order deciding an issue which, if decided in favour of the appellant, would be sufficient for the final disposal of the case.

133. Appellate jurisdiction of Supreme Court in appeals from High Courts in regard to civil matters.—(1) An appeal shall lie to the Supreme Court from any judgment, decree or final order in a civil proceeding of a High Court in the territory of India (if the High Court certifies under article 134A)—

(1) that the case involves a substantial question of law of general importance, and

(2) that in the opinion of the High Court the said question needs to be decided by the Supreme Court.

(2) Notwithstanding anything in article 132, any party appealing to the Supreme Court under clause (1) may urge as one of the grounds in such appeal that a substantial question of law as to the interpretation of this Constitution has been wrongly decided.

(3) Notwithstanding anything in this article, no appeal shall, unless Parliament by law otherwise provides, lie to the Supreme Court form the judgment, decree or final order of one Judge of a High Court.

134. Appellate jurisdiction of Supreme Court to criminal matters.—(1) An appeal shall lie to the Supreme Court from any judgment, final order or sentence in criminal proceeding of a High Court in the territory of India if the High Court—

(a) has on appeal reversed an order of acquittal of an accused person and sentenced him to death; or

(b) has withdrawn for trial before itself any case from any Court subordinate to its authority and has in such trial convicted the accused person and sentenced him to death; or

(c) (certifies under article 134A) that the case is a fit one for appeal to the Supreme Court:

Provided that an appeal under sub-clause (c) shall lie subject to such provisions as may be made in that behalf under clause (1) of article 145 and to such conditions as the High Court may establish or require.

(2) Parliament may by law confer on the Supreme Court any further powers to entertain and hear appeals from any judgment, final order or sentence in a criminal proceeding of a High Court in the territory of India subject to such conditions and limitations as may be specified in such law.

134A. Certificate for appeal to the Supreme Court.—Every High Court, passing or making a judgment, decree, final order, or sentence, referred to in clause (1) of article 132 or clause (1) of article 133, or clause (1) of article 134—

(a) may, if it deems fit so to do, on its own motion; and

(b) shall, if on oral application is made, by or on behalf of the party aggrieved, immediately after the passing or making of such judgment, decree, final order or sentence,

determine, as soon as may be after such passing or making, the question whether a certificate of the nature referred to in clause (1) of article 132, or clause (1) of article 133 or, as the case may be, sub-clause (c) of clause (1) of article 134, may be given in respect of that case.

135. Jurisdiction and powers of the Federal Court under existing law to be exercisable by the Supreme Court.—Until Parliament by law otherwise provides, the Supreme Court shall also have jurisdiction and powers with respect to any matter to which the provisions of article 133 or article 134 do not apply if jurisdiction and powers in relation to that matter were exercisable by the Federal Court immediately before the commencement of this Constitution under any existing law.

136. Special leave to appeal by the Supreme Court.—(1) Notwithstanding anything in this Chapter, the Supreme Court may, in its discretion, grant special leave to appeal from any judgment, decree, determination, sentence or order in any cause or matter passed or made by any Court or Tribunal in the territory of India.

(2) Nothing in clause (1) shall apply to any judgment, determination, sentence or order passed or made by any court or tribunal constituted by or under any law relating to the Armed Forces.

137. Review of judgments or orders by the Supreme Court.—Subject to the provisions of any law made by Parliament or any rules made under article 145, the Supreme Court shall have power to review any judgment pronounced or order made by it.

138. Enlargement of the jurisdiction of the Supreme Court.—(1) The Supreme court shall have such further jurisdiction and powers with respect to any of the matters in the Union List as Parliament may by law confer.

(2) The Supreme Court shall have such further jurisdiction and powers with respect to any matter as the Government of India and the Government of any State may by special agreement confer, if Parliament by law provides for the exercise of such jurisdiction and powers by the Supreme Court.

139. Conferment on the Supreme Court of powers to issue certain writs.—Parliament may by law confer on the Supreme Court power to issue directions, orders or writs, including writs in the nature of *habeas corpus, mandamus,* prohibition, *quo warranto* and *certiorari*, or any of them, for any purposes other than those mentioned in clause (2) of article 32.

139A. Transfer of certain cases.—(1) Where cases involving the same or substantially the same questions of law are pending before the Supreme Court and one or more High Courts or before two or more High Courts and the Supreme Court is satisfied on its own motion or any application made by the Attorney-General of India or by a party to any such case that such questions are substantial questions of general importance, the Supreme Court may withdraw the case or cases pending before the High Court or the High Courts and dispose of all the cases itself:

Provided that the Supreme Court may after determining the said questions of law return any case so withdrawn together with a copy of its judgment on such questions to the High Court from which the case has been withdrawn, and the High Court shall on receipt thereof, proceed to dispose of the case in conformity with such judgment.

(2) The Supreme Court may, if it deems it expedient so to do for the ends of justice, transfer any case, appeal or other proceedings pending before any High Court to any other High Court.

140. Ancillary powers of Supreme Court.—Parliament may by law make provisions for conferring upon the Supreme Court such supplemental powers not inconsistent with any of the provisions of this Constitution as may appear to be necessary or desirable for the purpose of enabling the court more effectively to exercise the jurisdiction conferred upon it by or under this Constitution.

141. Law declared by Supreme Court to be binding on all Courts.—The law declared by the Supreme Court shall be binding on all Courts within the territory of India.

142. Enforcement of decrees and orders of Supreme Court and orders as to discovery, etc.—(1) The Supreme Court in the exercise of its jurisdiction may pass such decree or make such order as is necessary for doing complete justice in any cause or matter pending before it, and any decree so passed or order so made shall be enforceable throughout the territory of India in such manner as may be prescribed by or under any law made by Parliament and, until provision in that behalf is so made, in such manner as the President may by order prescribe.

(2) Subject to the provisions of any law made in this behalf by Parliament, the Supreme Court shall, as respects the whole of the territory of India, have all and every power to make any order for the purpose of securing the attendance of any person, the discovery or production of any documents, or the investigation or punishment of any contempt of itself.

143. Power of President to consult Supreme Court.—(1) If at any time it appears to the President that a question of law or fact has arisen, or is likely to arise, which is of such a nature and of such public importance that it is expedient to obtain the opinion of the Supreme Court upon it, he may refer the question to that Court for consideration and the Court may, after such hearing as it thinks fit, report to the President its opinion thereon.

(2) The President may, notwithstanding anything in the proviso to article 131, refer a dispute of the kind mentioned in the said proviso to the Supreme Court for opinion and the Supreme Court shall, after such hearing as it thinks fit, report to the President its opinion thereon.

144. Civil and judicial authorities to act in aid of the Supreme Court.—All authorities, civil and judicial, in the territory of India shall act in aid of the Supreme Court.

144A. Special provisions as to disposal of questions relating to constitutional validity of laws.—[Rep. by Constitution (Forty-third Amendment) Act, 1977, sec. 5 w.e.f. 13-4-1978)]

145. Rules of Court, etc.—(1) Subject to the provisions of any law made by Parliament, the Supreme Court may from time to time, with the approval of the President, make rules for regulating generally the practice and procedure of the Court including—

(a) rules as to the persons practicing before the Court;

(b) rules as to the procedure for hearing appeals and other matters pertaining to appeals including the time within which appeals to the Court are to be entered;

(c) rules as to the proceedings in the Court for the enforcement of any of the rights conferred by Part III

(cc) rules as to the proceedings in the Court under (article 139A)

(d) rules as to the entertainment of appeals under sub-clause (c) of clause (1) of article 134;

(e) rules as to the conditions subject to which any judgment pronounced or order made by the Court may be reviewed and the procedure for such review including the time within which applications to the Court for such review are to be entered;

(f) rules as to the costs of and incidental to any proceedings in the Court and as to the fees to be charged in respect of proceedings therein;

(g) rules as to the granting bail;

(h) rules as to stay of proceedings;

(i) rules providing for the summary determination of any appeal which appears to the Court to be frivolous or vexatious or brought for the purpose of delay;

(j) rules as to the procedure for inquiries referred to in clause (1) of article 317.

(2) Subject to the provisions of clause (3), rules made under this article may fix the minimum number of Judges who are to sit for any purpose, and may provide for the powers of Single Judges and Division Courts.

(3) The minimum number of judges who are to sit for the purpose of deciding any case involving a substantial question of law as to the interpretation of this Constitution or for the purpose of hearing any reference under article 143 shall be five:

Provided that, where the Court hearing an appeal under any of the provisions of this Chapter other than article 132 consists of less than five judges and in the course of the hearing of the appeal the Court is satisfied that the appeal involves a substantial question of law as to the interpretation of this Constitution the determination of which is necessary for the disposal of the appeal, such Court shall refer the question for opinion to the Court constituted as required by this clause for the purpose of deciding any case involving such a question and shall on receipt of the opinion dispose of the appeal in conformity with such opinion.

(4) No judgment shall delivered by the Supreme Court save in open Court, and no report shall be made under article 143 save in accordance with an opinion also delivered in open Court.

(5) No judgment and no such opinion shall be delivered by the Supreme Court with the concurrence of a majority of the Judges present at the hearing of the case, but nothing in this clause shall be deemed to prevent a judge who does not concur from delivering a dissenting judgment or opinion.

146. Officers and servants and the expenses of the Supreme Court.—(1) Appointments of officers and servants of the Supreme Court shall be made by the Chief Justice of India or such other Judge or officer of the Court as he may direct:

Provided that the President may by rule require that in such cases as may be specified in the rule, no person not already attached to the Court shall be appointed to any office connected with the Court, save after consultation with the Union Public Service Commission.

(2) Subject to the provisions of any law made by Parliament, the conditions of service of officers and servants of the Supreme Court shall be such as may be prescribed by rules made by the Chief Justice of India or by some other Judge or officers of the Court authorized by the Chief Justice of India to make rules for the purpose:

Provided that the rules made under this clause shall, so far as they relate to salaries, allowances, leave or pension, require the approval of the President.

(3) The administrative expenses of the Supreme Court, including all salaries, allowances and pensions payable to or in respect of the officers and servants of the Court, shall be charged upon the Consolidated Fund of India, and any fees or other moneys taken by the Court shall form part of that Fund.

147. Interpretation.—In this Chapter and in Chapter V of Part VI, references to any substantial question of law as to the interpretation of this Constitution shall be construed as including references to any substantial question of law as to the interpretation of the Government of India Act, 1935 (including any enactment amending or supplementing that Act), or of any Order in Council or order made thereunder, or of the Indian Independence Act, 1947, or of any order made thereunder.

PART VIII

LIST OF THE JUDGES OF SUPREME COURT OF INDIA AS ON 1-5-2015

Sanctioned judge strength: 31

(List of Judges arranged according to date of appointment)

Sl. No.	Name of the judge S/Shri Justice	Date of Appointment	Date of Retirement	Remarks [Parent High Court]
1	Tirath Singh Thakur	17-11-2009	3-1-2017	CJI w.e.f. 3-12-2015 Jammu & Kashmir
2	Anil Ramesh Dave	30-4-2010	18-11-2016	Gujarat
3	Jagdish Singh Khehar	13-9-2011	27-8-2017	Punjab & Haryana
4	Dipak Misra	10-10-2011	2-10-2018	Orissa
5	Jasti Chelameswar	10-10-2011	22-6-2018	Andhra Pradesh
6	F.M.I. Kalifulla	02-4-2012	22-7-2016	Madras
7	Ranjan Gogoi	23-4-2012	17-11-2019	Gauhati
8	Madan Bhimarao Lokur	4-6-2012	30-12-2018	Delhi
9	M. Yusuf Eqbal	24-12-2012	12-2-2016	Jharkhand
10	V. Gopalagowda	24-12-2012	5-10-2016	Karnataka
11	Vikramajit Sen	24-12-2012	30-12-2015	Delhi
12	Pinaki Chandra Ghose	08-3-2013	27-5-2017	Calcutta
13	Kurian Joseph	08-3-2013	29-11-2018	Kerala
14	Arjan Kumar Sikri	12-4-2013	6-3-2019	Delhi
15	Sharad Arvind Bobde	12-4-2013	23-4-2021	Bombay
16	Shiva Kirti Singh	19-9-2013	12-11-2016	Patna
17	Chockalingam Nagappan	19-9-2013	3-10-2016	Madras
18	Rajesh Kumar Agrawal	17-2-2014	4-5-2018	Allahabad
19	Nuthalapati Venkata Ramana	17-2-2014	26-8-2022	Andhra Pradesh

Sl. No.	Name of the judge S/Shri Justice	Date of Appointment	Date of Retirement	Remarks [Parent High Court]
20	Arun Kumar Mishra	7-7-2014	2-9-2020	Madhya Pradesh
21	Adarsh Kumar Goel	7-7-2014	6-7-2018	Punjab & Haryana
22	Rohinton Fali Nariman	7-7-2014	12-8-2021	Bar
23	Abhay Manohar Sapre	13-8-2014	27-8-2019	Madhya Pradesh
24	Smt. R. Banumathi	13-8-2014	19-7-2020	Madras
25	Prafulla Chandra Pant	13-8-2014	29-8-2017	Uttarakhand
26	Uday Umesh Lalit	13-8-2014	8-11-2022	Bar
27	Amitava Roy	27-2-2015	28-2-2018	Gauhati

PART IX

THE IMPORTANT ROLE PLAYED BY SUPREME COURT IN EXERCISE OF POWERS OF JUDICIAL REVIEW UNDER CONSTITUTION FROM INCEPTION TO THE PRESENT DAY

The juristic basis of judicial review is the doctrine of *ultra vires*[1]. The concept of judicial review of legislation[2] was firmly evolved for the first time by Chief Justice Marshall in 1803 in *Marbury* v. *Madison*[3]. Emphasizing that a Constitution is paramount law, Justice Marshal said:

> "It is emphatically the province and duty of the judicial department to say what the law is........If two laws conflict with each other, the Courts must decide on the operation of each.......If, then, the Courts are to regard the Constitution and the Constitution is superior to any ordinary Act of the Legislature, the Constitution, and not such ordinary Act, must govern the case to which they both apply."

Any declaration otherwise, the Chief Justice concluded:

> ".....would be subversive of the very foundation of all written Constitutions, would force the Judges to close their eyes to the Constitution, and would make the judicial oath "a solemn mockery". (18) Edward S. Corwin: *Op.Cit.*, p. 559".

---

1. Lord Browne – Wilkinson in *Boddington* v. *British Transport Police,* (1999) 2 SCC 143 (164).
2. See *Sakinala Harinath* v. *State of Andhra Pradesh,* 1993 SCC Online AP 195 at paras 36, 37.
3. 2 L.Ed 60: 5 US (1 Cr) 137 (1803).

Lord Dyson, Master of the Rolls, has said judicial review of administrative action is the fundamental means by which a democracy makes good its commitment to the rule of law. The ability of those affected by decisions taken by public bodies, State officials, and those who are empowered to carry public functions on behalf of the State, to hold them to account and to ensure that they act according to the law, is the lifeblood of a just society.

In India, the power of judicial review by the Courts is derived from the Constitution itself. Articles 32 and 226 of the Constitution of India provide the right to approach the Supreme Court and the High Courts for enforcement of their fundamental rights guaranteed under Part III of the Constitution of India. Thus, the Supreme Court and the High Courts in exercise of such powers are not restrained by the narrow concept of judicial review prevalent under the English administrative law. In the Indian context Judicial Review would be the judicial scrutiny of legislative, administrative or state action on the touchstone of the Constitution.

From the nature of the powers conferred by the Constitution on the Supreme Court and the High Courts, it is axiomatic that they are the sole repositories of the power of judicial review. Power of judicial review implies the power to interpret and enforce the Constitution and this power includes the power to pronounce upon the validity of statutes, actions taken and orders passed by individuals and bodies falling within the ambit of the expression 'State' occurring in Article 12 or performing or carrying out public functions referred to as 'other authorities' in Article 226[4]. In a democratic set up governed by a written Constitution, judicial review is the most effective instrument to ensure that the Legislature and the Executive do not transgress the limitations imposed by the Constitution.

It is pertinent to note here the importance of such powers conferred on the Constitutional Courts[5]. While expressing his views on the significance of draft Article 25, which corresponds to the present Article 32 of the Constitution, Dr. B.R. Ambedkar,

---

4. *Sukhdev Singh* v. *Bhagatram,* (1975) 1 SCC 421.
5. See *L. Chandra Kumar* v. *Union of India,* (1997) 3 SCC 261 (299) at para 73.

the Chairman of the Drafting Committee of the Constituent Assembly stated as follows: (CAD, Vol. VII, p. 953)

> "If I was asked to name any particular article in this Constitution as the most important — an article without which this Constitution would be a nullity — I could not refer to any other article except this one. It is the very soul of the Constitution and the very heart of it and I am glad that the House has realised its importance."
> (emphasis added)

This statement of Dr. Ambedkar has been specifically reiterated in several judgments of the Hon'ble Supreme Court to emphasise the unique significance attributed to Article 32 in our constitutional scheme.[6]

The legitimacy of the power of Courts within constitutional democracies to review legislative action has been questioned since the time it was first conceived. The Constitution of India, being alive to such criticism, has, while conferring such power upon the higher Judiciary, incorporated important safeguards. The Judges of the superior courts have been entrusted with the task of upholding the Constitution and to this end, have been conferred the power to interpret it. It is they who have to ensure that the balance of power envisaged by the Constitution is maintained and that the legislature and the executive do not, in the discharge of their functions, transgress constitutional limitations. The power of judicial review over legislative action vested in the High Courts under Article 226 and in the Supreme Court under Article 32 of the Constitution is an integral and essential feature of the Constitution, constituting part of its basic structure.[7] The Supreme Court has gone on to hold that the power to test the validity of legislations against the provisions of the Constitution can be conferred even upon Administrative Tribunals created under the Act or upon Tribunals created under Article 323B of the Constitution.

The scope and extent of power of the judicial review of the High Court contained in Article 226 of the Constitution of India

---

6. [*See* for instance, Khanna, J. in *Kesavananda Bharati* case, (1973) 4 SCC 225 (p. 818), Bhagwati, J. in *Minerva Mills,* (1980) 3 SCC 625 (678), Chandrachud, C.J. in *Fertilizer Corporation Kamgar Union (Regd.)* v. *Union of India,* (1981) 1 SCC 568 (para 11), R. Misra, J. in *Sampath Kumar,* (1987) 1 SCC 124: (1987) 2 ATC 82 (137).]
7. See *L. Chandra Kumar* v. *Union of India,* (1997) 3 SCC 261 at paras 78, 79 following *Kesavananda Bharti* case.

would vary from case-to-case, the nature of the order, the relevant statute as also the other relevant factors including the nature of power exercised by the public authorities, namely, whether the power is statutory, *quasi*-judicial or administrative. The power of judicial review is not intended to assume a supervisory role or done the robes of *omnipresent*[8]. The power of judicial review by the High Court under Article 226 is significantly wider than the power of the Supreme Court under Article 32.

Traditionally, the Courts exercised their powers of judicial review in a narrow sense for striking down legislations on the ground of violation of fundamental rights and/or *ultra vires* of the Constitution; and administrative actions and orders on the grounds of arbitrariness and unreasonableness as enshrined under Article 14 of the Constitution. Despite the same, Courts were still reluctant to strike down provisions of the Constitution. The Supreme Court in some early decisions held that Article 368 provided the Parliament with unlimited power to amend the Constitution[9] thereby establishing supremacy of Parliament over the Constitution. However, in *Golak Nath* case[10], Chief Justice Subba Rao speaking for the majority, by invoking the doctrine of implied limitations on the power to amend, held that the Parliament's power to amend the Constitution could not be used to abridge fundamental rights and further applied the doctrine of prospective over-ruling.

The impact of judicial review was further felt in the *Bank Nationalization* case[11] where the Supreme Court by a majority of 10:1, held the challenge to the ordinance for nationalization of banks by the Government as an unreasonable restriction and *ultra vires* the Constitution.

In *Kesavananda Bharti* case[12], the Supreme Court by a majority of 7:6, overruled the decision in *Golak Nath* case (supra) by holding that no amendment could be made to alter the basic structure of the Constitution. Thus came to be evolved the doctrine of basic structure, which to this day is the core

8. See *State of Uttar Pradesh* v. *Johri Mal,* (2004) 4 SCC 714 at para 28.
9. *Shankari Prasad Singh Deo* v. *Union of India,* AIR 1951 SC 458; *Sajjan Singh* v. *State of Rajasthan,* AIR 1965 SC 845.
10. *Golak Nath* v. *State of Punjab,* AIR 1967 SC 1643.
11. *R.C. Cooper* v. *Union of India,* (1970) 1 SCC 248.
12. *Kesavananda Bharti* v. *State of Kerala,* (1973) 4 SCC 225.

of Constitutional interpretation. The basic structure doctrine was followed to strike down the 39th Amendment to the Constitution which was sought to be introduced to validate the election of Mrs. Gandhi[13] pending challenge to such election before the Allahabad High Court. Judicial Review thus played an important role and the Courts were regarded as the preservers of the Constitution.

However, in *ADM, Jabalpur* v. *Shivakant Shukla*[14], the Hon'ble Supreme Court by a majority of 4 : 1, held that the right of a person to approach the High Court for judicial review under Article 226 could be suspended during the proclamation of emergency under Article 352 of the Constitution. The lone dissenter in this judgment, Justice Khanna, is still hailed to this day to have reflected the true spirit of the Constitution in his dissenting judgment.

Post-emergency, the Courts took upon themselves a more activist and social approach and in Justice Goswami's words, became "the last resort for the bewildered and the oppressed".[15]

The rigid traditional approach of locus and the aggrieved party approaching the Court was relaxed and the doors to writ jurisdiction were thrown open to the socially and economically backward sections of the society for their benefit[16] and thus marked the beginning of PILs in India. Justices Krishna Iyer and Bhagwati were pioneers of this era and entertained public spirited citizens to approach the Courts with grievances regarding environment, human rights, etc.

In the 90's, the Courts started entertaining PILs relating to environmental issues and started monitoring various issues such as pollution, protection and conservation of forests, vehicular pollution, etc.[17] Recently, issues concerning environmental degradation, preservation of ecology, inter-generational equity

13. *Indira Nehru Gandhi* v. *Raj Narain*, 1975 Supp SCC 1.
14. (1976) 2 SCC 521.
15. *State of Rajasthan* v. *Union of India*, (1977) 3 SCC 592.
16. *Fertilizer Corporation Kamgar Union (Regd.)* v. Union *of India*, (1981) 1 SCC 568; *S.P. Gupta* v. *Union of India*, (1981) Supp SCC 87; *Bhandua Mukti Morcha* v. *Union of India*, AIR 1984 SC 802: (1984) 3 SCC 161.
17. *Vellore Citizens Welfare Forum* v. *Union of India*, (1996) 5 SCC 647; *T.N. Godavarman* v. *Union of India*, (1997) 2 SCC 267; (1998) 2 SCC 341; *M.C. Mehta* v. *Union of India*, (1997) 2 SCC 353, etc.

and such other concepts have also come to be recognized by the Courts in PILs on environmental issues. Illegal mining causing harm to the environment and loss to the public exchequer have been brought to the notice of the Courts which have heavily come down on such day light robbery.

In recent times, judicial review of administrative action has become expansive and is becoming wider day-by-day. The majority in *S.R. Bommai* v. *Union of India*[18] case held that the subjective satisfaction of the President in issuing a proclamation under Article 356 is also subject to judicial review.

The traditionalistic and conservative approach by the Courts in exercising powers of judicial review has been vanishing and the sphere of judicial scrutiny is being expanded. State activity too is becoming fast pervasive. As the State has descended into the commercial field and giant public sector undertakings have come up, the stake of the public exchequer is also large justifying larger social audit, judicial control and review by opening of the public gaze[19]. Though in *stricto sensu,* the courts ordinarily refrain from digressing into policy decisions in exercise of judicial review, the Supreme Court and the High Courts have judiciously exercised their discretion to enter into such domains in the larger public interests.

In the *2G Spectrum Allocation* case[20], while acknowledging that the scope of judicial review in policy matters is limited, the Supreme Court went on to rule that when it is clearly demonstrated that the policy framed by the State or its agency/instrumentality and/or its implementation is contrary to public interest or is violative of the constitutional principles, it is the duty of the Court to exercise its jurisdiction in larger public interest and reject the stock plea of the State that the scope of judicial review should not be exceeded beyond the recognised parameters. Terming the allocation of 2G Spectrum licenses as illegal, the Supreme Court minced no words while observing that an important national asset was virtually gifted away at throwaway prices following the "first-come-first-serve' policy and that if the method of auction had been adopted for grant

18. (1994) 3 SCC 1.
19. *Star Enterprises* v. *City and Industrial Development Corpn. of Maharashtra Ltd.,* (1990) 3 SCC 280 (284) para 10.
20. *CPIL* v. *Union of India,* (2012) 3 SCC 1.

of licence, which could be the only rational transparent method for distribution of national wealth, the nation would have been enriched by many thousand crores. However, in *Natural Resources Allocation Reference*[21], the Court observed that the methodology pertaining to disposal of natural resources is clearly an economic policy and Courts cannot mandate the method of auction to be followed in all cases. At the same time, reaffirming its power of judicial review, the Court added that it is entitled to analyse the legal validity of different means of distribution and give a constitutional answer as to which methods are *ultra vires* and *intra vires* the Constitution. While it cannot compare which policy is fairer than the other, but if a policy or law is patently unfair to the extent that it falls foul of the fairness requirement of Article 14 of the Constitution, the Court would not hesitate in striking it down.

Similarly, in the more recent judgment terming allocation of coal blocks as illegal[22], the Supreme Court observed that the entire process of allocation suffered from the vice of arbitrariness and legal flaws. The Bench, of which Justice Lokur was also a part, held that the Screening Committee's approach was *ad hoc* and casual; it did not act in a consistent or transparent manner, there was no proper application of mind, and it was seldom guided by relevant factors. Further the Bench observed that there was no criteria, let alone objective criteria for evaluation of comparative merits.

Though there was no specific ruling of the Court on the power of judicial review, it referred to the observation in the Natural Resources Allocation Reference that judicial scrutiny of methods of disposal of natural resources should depend on the facts and circumstances of each case, and when such a policy decision is not backed by a social or welfare purpose and scarce natural resources are alienated for commercial pursuits of profit maximising private entrepreneurs, the Court, in exercise of power of judicial review, shall term the Executive action as arbitrary, unfair, unreasonable and capricious due to its antimony with Article 14.

---

21. *Natural Resources Allocation, In re, Special Reference No. 1 of 2012,* (2010) 10 SCC 1.
22. *Manohar Lal Sharma* v. *The Principal Secretary,* Writ Petition (CRL.) No. 120 of 2012, judgment dated 25-8-2014.

Where the investigating agencies have failed to perform their duties such as in the 2G and the Coal-block allocation cases, the Courts have under judicial review assumed the role of monitoring investigations done by such agencies. Such extraordinary exercise of powers by the Courts have ensured fair, independent and timely investigations.

Pursuant to the orders passed in a PIL by the Hon'ble Supreme Court regarding Black Money[23] stashed in foreign banks, the Government has set-up a Special Investigation Team (SIT) comprising two former judges of the Hon'ble Supreme Court to oversee and investigate into the monies of Indian Nationals lying in such foreign banks.

A Constitution Bench of the Supreme Court in a recent judgment has struck down section 6A of the Delhi Special Police Establishment Act, 1946 which provided for mandatorily seeking prior permission for investigation of persons of the rank of joint secretary and above. Chief Justice Lodha speaking for the Bench said:

> "This provision on the face of it is not valid. It grants absolute protection to corrupt officers from prosecution. They don't need a shield like this merely because they are likely to be harassed."

The Bench pointed to the discrimination that was caused between Central Government Officers working at the level of Joint Secretary and above and the same level officers working in the States. The Court said that corrupt persons ought to be treated equally under the Prevention of Corruption Act and warned of serious consequences if any inquiry is hampered.

In the *Lily Thomas* case[24], the Supreme Court while striking down section 8(4) of the Representation of Peoples Act, 1951 as *ultra vires* the Constitution, held that the Legislature/ Parliament had no power to enact a law whereby a conviction of a member of the House was postponed by 3 months. Once again this resulted in a proposal for an ordinance to be issued to nullify the effect of such judgment. However, public opinion prevailed and the law declared by the Supreme Court remained intact and the proposed Ordinance never saw the light of day.

23. *Ram Jethmalani* v. *Union of India,* (2011) 8 SCC 1.
24. *Lily Thomas* v. *Union of India,* (2013) 7 SCC 653.

Critics have been wary of the fact that while widening the scope of judicial review the Courts have even struck down various legislations on the grounds of arbitrariness, unreasonableness and *mala fides;* interfered with policy decisions; etc. In fact further criticism is accorded to the Constitutional Courts that judicial review has led to an over activist Judiciary.

However, it is my firm belief that such activism has always been on the touchstone of the Constitution. In fact the most recent judgment of the Constitution Bench of the Supreme Court in *Manoj Narula* v. *Union of India,*[25] on the issue of persons with criminal antecedents and/or backgrounds being appointed as Ministers, is a testimony to the fact that the Courts would not assume jurisdiction blindly in the guise of judicial review where none exists. The Court rejected the contention of applying the doctrine of implied limitation for the purposes of limiting the discretion of the Prime Minister to advise the President on appointment of Ministers. The Court refused to lay down law in the absence of any specific provisions in the Constitution in this regard. Further Justice Lokur in his separate concurring judgment has said that the expression 'criminal antecedents' or 'criminal background' is extremely vague and incapable of any precise definition. He has further observed that though it may be necessary, due to the criminalization of our polity and consequently of our politics, to ensure that certain persons do not become Ministers, this would not be possible through guidelines issued by the Court and that it is for the electorate to ensure that suitable persons are elected to the Legislature and it is for the Legislature to enact or not enact a more restrictive law.

Before concluding, I would like to deviate into another aspect which I thought would be relevant, including the problems which arise before Courts in enforcement of socio-economic rights.

The jurisprudential question explores the nature of socio-economic rights and their formulation by the Courts for their enforcement. The distinction between duties of restraint and positive duties, although controversial, is said to underline the debate of enforcement of socio-economic rights. Civil and political rights giving rise to negative duties or duties of restraint

25. Writ Petition (Civil) No. 289 of 2005, delivered on 27th August, 2014.

are considered immediate, resource free and determinate thereby more amenable to judicial resolution while socio-economic rights giving rise to positive duties are considered indeterminate, programmatic and requiring resources, thereby best left to the political process. Therefore, the distinction between action and omission of action underlies the distinction between positive and negative rights and skews the debate to a simplistic bipolar understanding of a rather holistic set of human rights.

The traditional notion of socio-economic rights mainly points to the institutional limitations of Courts, which undermine their competence to make decisions with policy implications and resource consequences. Concerns over institutional capacity raise questions as to whether there are judicially discoverable and manageable standards for resolving such socio-economic issues. These issues often require significant expertise and are commonly regarded as unsuitable for judicial resolution. Institutional legitimacy, in contrast, refers to the democratic objection to the justiciability of socio-economic rights drawn from the view that certain issues are said to be best left to politically accountable branches of Government, rather than an unelected judiciary, regardless of judicial capacity considerations.

These concerns have been overwhelmingly significant in the enforcement of socio-economic rights and the Courts themselves have been gripped of its importance in India. Pathak J. in *Bandhua Mukti Morcha*[26] had cautioned against the trappings of judicial enforcement of SER saying:

> "... there is always the possibility ... of succumbing to the legislature or to the executive government... In the process of correcting executive error or removing legislative omission the Court can so easily find itself involved in policy-making of a quality and to a degree characteristic of political authority and indeed run the risk of being mistaken for one"

These concerns demonstrate why, in determining when socio-economic rights should be considered justiciable by the courts, regards must be had to the theory of democracy. A workable institutional approach views the three organs of the State, not in conflict but rather complementary to each other.

26. AIR 1984 SC 802: (1984) 3 SCC 161.

- **Minimum Core Obligations**

Although the Supreme Court is aware that enforcement of socio-economic rights involves matters of policy best left to other branches, it has overcome theoretical obstacles to promote justice and has been able to carve out the core content of the right that calls for action irrespective of the economic capacity of the State. For instance, the Supreme Court, in *Unnikrishnan J.P.* v. *State of Andhra Pradesh*[27], identified the right to free primary education up to the age of 14 as the core minimum of the right to education while in *Paschim Banga Khet Mazdoor Samity* v. *State of West Bengal*[28], the right to emergency medical care as the core of the right to health. The concept of minimum core is useful in contextualizing the role of Courts amidst the debate of justiciability of socio-economic rights as it carves out an immediate and determinate goal for an otherwise progressively realisable right. Lack of financial resources is also not recognized as a justification for defining the core minimum content of the right. Although defining the minimum core is in itself a difficult process but it seems to be a pragmatic solution to meet the ends of justice and make the judicial process more meaningful.

The Supreme Court of India declared that the right to life enshrined in the Indian Constitution (Article 21) imposes an obligation on the State to safeguard the right to life of every person and that preservation of human life is of paramount importance. This obligation on the State stands irrespective of constraints in financial resources. The Court stated that denial of timely medical treatment necessary to preserve human life in government-owned hospitals is a violation of this right. The Court asked the Government of West Bengal to pay the petitioner compensation for the loss suffered. It also directed the Government to formulate a blue print for primary health care with particular reference to treatment of patients during an emergency.

The problems with minimum core have been articulated by the South African Constitutional Court in the case of *Government of South Africa* v. *Grootboom*[29] asserting that (i) it would be difficult to determine in the abstract what the minimum threshold should

27. (1993) 1 SCC 645.
28. (1996) 4 SCC 37.
29. (2000) 11 BCLR 1169.

be for the realization of the right, as the opportunities for fulfilling these rights varied considerably and the needs were diverse; (ii) determining the minimum core for a particular right requires a great deal of information to which the Courts often do not have access; and (iii) Courts are not institutionally equipped to make the wide-ranging factual and political inquiries necessary for determining what the minimum core standard should be.

- **Positive Duties arising from 'negative' rights**

The case of *Olga Tellis* v. *Bombay Municipal Corporation*[30] shows us that socio-economic rights can be formulated negatively when the right to housing was defined in terms of freedom from State interference by protecting the right of pavement dwellers through procedural due process while facing forced evictions. The case is interesting since although the Court declined to provide the remedies requested by the petitioners the Court held that the right to life ("negative") under Article 21 of the Indian Constitution encompassed the right to livelihood.

In *Shantistar Builders* v. *Narayan Khimalal Totame*[31], the right to a reasonable accommodation to live in was read into the right to life, wherein the Supreme Court of India had held that a reasonable residence is an indispensable necessity for fulfilment of the constitutional goal in the matter of development of man and should be taken as included in 'life' in Article 21. This obligation was extended in *Ahmedabad Municipal Corporation* v. *Nawab Khan Gulba Khan*[32], where the Court had stated that "it is the duty of the State to construct houses at reasonable rates and make them easily accessible to the poor."

- **Continuing *Mandamus***

In the Right to Food cases, the Hon'ble Supreme Court has already recognized a fundamental right to food and the right to freedom from malnutrition has also been acknowledged[33]. But, how does one enforce a fundamental right, which by its very nature, is not a one-time right, but continues throughout the life of the individual. It is for this reason that the Court has devised an innovative remedy, the writ of continuing *mandamus*,

30. 1985 (2) Supp SCR 51.
31. (1990) 1 SCC 520.
32. (1997) 11 SCC 121.
33. *PUCL* v. *Union of India*, 2005 AIR SCW 3125.

whereby the inherently programmatic socio-economic right to food is implemented, not through the issuance of a one-time order, but through constant directions at repeated intervals.

Reference is invited to Justice Bhagwati's words in the *S.P. Gupta* case[34]:

> "...... If there is one principle which runs through the entire fabric of the Constitution, it is the principle of the rule of law and under the Constitution, it is the Judiciary which is entrusted with the task of keeping every organ of the State within the limits of the law and thereby making the rule of law meaningful and effective. It is to aid the Judiciary in this task that the power of judicial review has been conferred upon the Judiciary and it is by exercising this power which constitutes one of the most potent weapons in armory of the law, that the Judiciary seeks to protect the citizen against violation of his constitutional or legal rights or misuse or abuse of power by the State or its officers......"

[Speech delivered by Shri Mohan Prasaran, Senior Advocate (former Solicitor-General of India) in the Hon'ble Delhi High Court on 29.8.2014.]

34. *S.P. Gupta* v. *Union of India,* (1981) Supp SCC 87.

PART X

PROLOGUE AND EPILOGUE, SUPREME COURT OF UK

CHAPTER I

FORMATION OF SUPREME COURT OF UK

The UK's first Supreme Court came into being on Thursday, 1.10.2009 with the swearing-in of 11 judges, replacing the House of Lords as the highest appeal Tribunal, a move aimed at establishing judicial independence in the country. Eleven new justices took their oaths of office in the new Supreme Court building across Parliament Square in Central London at a function attended among others by India's Law Minister M. Veerappa Moily. Since 1876, Law Lords in the House of Lords, the Upper House of the British Parliament, used to perform the role of final Court of appeal for England, Wales and Northern Ireland.

The Court is independent body and will hear the most important cases, thereby it is different from the earlier conventions where legislature used to enjoy judicial powers. After his swearing-in, Nicholas Phillips, the President of the Supreme Court, said that the move was important for "judicial independence". He said that "This is the last step in the separation of powers in this country. We have come to the point where the judges are separated from the legislature and executive".

There are many examples which shows that status of justice in England.

Let it be the judges. The words of lord Denning, a great if flawed judge, were controversial when he uttered them 30 years ago. Back in 1980, Lord Denning was speaking defensively: admirers and foes saw the Judiciary as the Establishment in ermine. The criminal justice system was about to enter years of agony the wrenching change as police wrongdoing was exposed, especially in the obtaining of confessions, and big terrorist convictions were overturned. But his injunction now looks rather prescient.

Today, answering Lord Denning's plea three decades late, a country drowning in distrust has fastened onto the Judiciary and its works as a source of redress. After every calamity – whether a terrorist attack, a police shooting, killings in Iraq or a royal death – the clamor rises for inquiries headed by a judge, with the power to quiz witnesses under oath.

Inquiries of one sort or another seem to be everywhere. On October 11th Britain's press covered the opening of an inquest into the London bus and Tube bombings of July 7th 2005. The bomb attacks have been probed in a criminal trial and parliamentary investigations. But bereaved families want the inquest – headed by the High Court Judge – to examine whether the domestic security service, M15, could have prevented the attacks, and whether emergency services were slow to respond.

On the same day the press reported fresh demands for a public inquiry into the killing of six British military policemen in Iraq in 2003, after a trial of alleged perpetrators collapsed in Baghdad. Interviewed by a newspaper, a Democratic Unionist MP from Northern Ireland appeared to launch an inquiries bidding war. Britain had spent 200m pounds ($320m) on the 12 years Seville Inquiry into the 1972 "Bloody Sunday" shootings of protesters by British paratroops, in Londonderry, he claimed, yet could not afford "justice" for army families. On October 7th an inquest jury in London found that police had lawfully killed a Barrister as he fired a shotgun from the window of his flat, but in an extended "narrative verdict" said officers had given insufficient weight to the dead man's alcoholism. Press coverage was extensive but muted, after the widow stated that she respected the verdict.

Meanwhile, a formal inquiry into the Iraq war (the fifth by some counts) that began in July 2009 is continuing, headed by a retired Whitehall mandarin, Sir John Chilcot. Another, headed by Sir Prter Gibson, a former judge, will soon probe alleged collusion between British spooks and foreign tortures.

This is superficially puzzling. After all, by education, culture and habit, most judges are memories of Britain's despised, mistrusted ruling elite. Yet their reputation has rarely been higher.

People "want to know what happened", suggests Michael Mansfield, a Barrister and veteran of high-profile inquiries and inquests. What they seek is not retribution but those in authority to be "brought to book" by legal questioning. The bereaved want lessons learned, giving some meaning to their loss. And the public has no faith in the House of Commons – a noisy, jeering pit of partisan barracking, further undermined by the Parliamentary – expenses scandals – as a forum for establishing truth. Simultaneously, he says, there has been "a resurrection of faith" in the Judiciary, notably after judges in the House of Lords condemned moves by the previous government to detain or control terror suspects without charge, or on the basis of secret evidence.

Mr. Mansfield is a self-described "radical lawyer", unloved on the right. Thus analysis is echoed by a senior Conservative politician, who recalls when judges were seen as "lions under the throne": unholders of the system. Now, he says judges are seen as "unholders of the rule of law", curbing an over-mighty state.

Is today's inquiry mania sustainable? There are technical reasons why judges seem to be everywhere. Above all, the 1998 Human Rights Act enshrined the "right to life" – from Article 2 of the European Convention on Human Rights – into domestic law. That has transformed inquests, which must now consider not just who died, where and when, but "how" in its broadest sense. That may include deciding if public-policy lessons can be drawn from a death. The quality of inquests used to be hit and miss, with local lawyers and doctors serving as corners. Now, when a death has an "Article 2 dimension", a High Court judge is often drafted in as coroner, as in the July 7th terror inquest. What is more a growing number of claimants now seek – and obtain – judicial reviews of decision made by public bodies, with judges asked to ponder everything from terrorist control orders to planning decisions.

Judges know their prominence carries risks. They are partly filling a vacuum created by the vertiginous fall of elected politicians from grace. Just 13 per cent of respondents trusted politicians to tell the truth in a 2009 survey by Ipsos MORI (below even journalists). Judges were trusted by 80 per cent. British judges are appointed, not elected, and public trust is strongly bound up with their political independence. Lord Carlile, a Liberal Democrat peer and the government's independent reviewer of terrorism legislation worries that judges' findings are cheered when they chime with public opinion, but when they do not – as with the Hutton Inquiry into the death of the government weapons expert David Kelly – they are denounced as a "white wash". And the painful truth is that some decisions are properly taken by members of an elected executive. Senior judges are queasy about being asked to review terrorist control orders, for example.

The public's yearning for judicial resolution of every crisis risks dragging judges close to the realm of politics. Lord Denning was right: someone must be trusted. If Judges are not, who might take their place?

CHAPTER II

1st Hon'ble Judge of Supreme Court of UK

Lord Neuberger

President of the Supreme Court, The Right Hon'ble the Lord Neuberger of Abbotsbury, born on 10th January, 1948 Lord Neuberger was educated at Westminster School, later studied Chemistry at Christ Church, Oxford. After graduating he worked at the merchant bank, N.M. Rothschild & Sons from 1970-1973 until he entered Lincoln's Inn and was called to the Bar in 1974. He was made a Queen's Counsel in 1987 and became Bencher for Lincoln's Inn in 1993. His first judicial appointment was as a Recorder from 1990 until 1996 when he was appointed a High Court judge in the Chancery Division and was then the Supervisory Chancery Judge for the Midland, Wales and Chester and Western Circuits 2000-2004.

In 1999 Lord Neuberger chaired the Advisory Committee on the Spoliation of Art (in the Holocaust). Since 2000 he has been a governor of the University of Arts, London and in 2003 became the Chairman of the Schizophrenia Trust. In January, 2004 he was appointed a Lord Justice of Appeal. In 2007 he was made a Lord of Appeal in Ordinary and created a life peer as Baron Neuberger of Abbotsbury in the County of Dorset.

Lady Haleady Hale

Deputy President of The Supreme Court, The Right Hon'ble the Baroness Hale of Richmond

Lady Hale was appointed Deputy President of The Supreme Court in June, 2013, succeeding Lord Hope of Craighead. In January, 2004, Lady Hale became the United Kingdom's first woman Lord of Appeal in Ordinary after a varied career as an academic lawyer, law reformer, and judge. In October, 2009 she became the first woman Justice of The Supreme Court. After graduating from Cambridge in 1966, she taught law at Manchester University from 1966 to 1984, also qualifying as a Barrister and practicing for a while at the Manchester Bar. She specialised in Family and Social Welfare Law, was founding editor of the Journal of Social Welfare and Family Law, and authored a pioneering case book on 'The Family, Law and Society'. In 1984 she was the first woman to be appointed to the Law Commission, a statutory body which promotes the reform of the law. Important legislation resulting from the work of her team at the Commission includes the Children Act, 1989, The Family Law Act, 1996, and the Mental Capacity Act, 2005. She also began sitting as an assistant recorder. In 1994 she became a High Court judge. She retains her links with the academic world as Chancellor of the University of Bristol, Visitor of Girton College, Cambridge, and Visiting Professor of Kings College, London. A home-maker as well as a judge, she thoroughly enjoyed helping the artists and architects create a new home for The Supreme Court.

Lord Mance

Justice of The Supreme Court, The Right Hon'ble the Lord Mance

Lord Mance became a Lord of Appeal in Ordinary in 2005. He was from 1999 to 2005 a Lord Justice of Appeal and from 1993 to 1999 a Judge of the High Court, Queen's Bench Division, where he also sat in the Commercial Court. Lord Mance read law at University College, Oxford, spent time with a Hamburg law firm and then practised at the commercial Bar and sat as a Recorder until 1993. He chaired various Banking

Appeals Tribunals and was a founder director of the Bar Mutual Indemnity Insurance Fund.

He represented the United Kingdom on the Council of Europe's Consultative Council of European Judges from 2000 to 2011, being elected its first chair from 2000 to 2003. He currently chairs the Executive Council of the International Law Association and the Lord Chancellor's Advisory Committee on Private International Law. He is a member of the Judicial Integrity Group and of the seven person panel set-up under the Treaty on the Functioning of the European Union (article 255) to give an opinion on candidates' suitability to perform the duties of Judge and Advocate-General of the European Court of Justice and General Court.

He served from 2007 to 2009 on the House of Lords European Union Select Committee, chairing sub-committee E which scrutinises proposals concerning European law and institutions.

Lord Kerr

Justice of The Supreme Court, The Right Hon'ble the Lord Kerr of Tonaghmore

Lord Kerr served as Lord Chief Justice of Northern Ireland from 2004 to 2009, and was the last Lord of Appeal in Ordinary appointed before the creation of The Supreme Court. Lord Kerr was educated at St. Colman's College, Newry, and read law at Queen's University, Belfast. He was called to the Bar of Northern Ireland in 1970, and to the Bar of England and Wales at Gray's Inn in 1974.

He served as Junior Crown Counsel from 1978 to 1983, at which point he took silk and served as Senior Crown Counsel from 1988 to 1993. In 1993 he was appointed a Judge of the High Court and knighted. He became Lord Chief Justice and joined the Privy Council in 2004.

Lord Clarke

Justice of The Supreme Court, The Right Hon'ble the Lord Clarke of Stone-cum-Ebony

Lord Clarke spent 27 years at the Bar, specialising in maritime and commercial law, undertaking a wide variety of cases in these areas. He became a Recorder in 1985, sitting in both criminal and civil courts. He conducted the Marchioness and Bowbelle Inquiries and was appointed Master of the Rolls in 2005. He is the first Justice to be appointed directly to The Supreme Court.

He was appointed to the High Court Bench in 1993 and in April that year succeeded Mr. Justice Sheen as the Admiralty Judge. He also sat in the Commercial Court and the Crown Court trying commercial and criminal cases respectively. Appointed to the Court of Appeal in 1998, he was called upon to conduct first the Thames Safety Inquiry and in the following year the Marchioness and Bowbelle Inquiries. On 1st October, 2005 he was appointed Master of the Rolls and Head of Civil Justice.

Lord Wilson

Justice of The Supreme Court, The Right Hon'ble Lord Wilson of Culworth

In 1967, after reading jurisprudence at Worcester College, Oxford, Lord Wilson was called to the Bar of England and Wales; and for the next 26 years, first as a junior and ultimately in silk, he practised almost exclusively in the field of family law.

From 1993 until 2005 he was a judge of the Family Division of the High Court. From 2005 until May, 2011 he was a judge of the Court of Appeal.

In May, 2011 he became a Justice of The Supreme Court.

Lord Sumption

Justice of The Supreme Court, The Right Hon'ble Lord Sumption

After reading history at Magdalen College, Oxford, and serving for four years as a history Fellow of the College, Lord Sumption was called to the Bar (Inner Temple) in 1975 and took Silk in 1986. His practice covered all aspects of Commercial, EU and Competition, Public and Constitutional Law.

He was appointed as a Deputy High Court Judge in 1992 and served as a Recorder between 1993 and 2001. He was appointed as a Judge of the Courts of Appeal of Jersey and Guernsey in 1995. In January 2012 he became a Justice of The Supreme Court.

Lord Sumption was a Judicial Appointments Commissioner from 2006 to 2011. He is also an accomplished historian.

Lord Reed

Justice of The Supreme Court, The Right Hon'ble Lord Reed

Lord Reed is one of the two Scottish Justices of The Supreme Court. After studying law at the universities of Edinburgh and Oxford, he was admitted to the Faculty of Advocates in 1983, where he undertook a wide range of civil work.

He served as a senior judge in Scotland for 13 years, being appointed to the Outer House of the Court of Session in 1998 and promoted to the Inner House in January, 2008. During 1999 he sat as an *ad hoc* judge of the European Court of Human Rights.

Lord Carnwath

Justice of The Supreme Court, The Right Hon'ble Lord Carnwath of Notting Hill, CVO

After studying law at Trinity College, Cambridge, Lord Carnwath was called to the Bar (Middle Temple) in 1968 and took silk in 1985. He served as Attorney General to the Prince of Wales from 1988 to 1994.

He was a judge of the Chancery Division from 1994 to 2002, during which time (1998 to 2002) he was also Chairman of the Law Commission. Lord Carnwath was appointed to the Court of Appeal in 2002.

Between 2007 and 2012 he was Senior President of Tribunals and led the planning and implementation of the reforms of the Tribunal system following the Leggatt report.

Lord Hughes

Justice of The Supreme Court, The Right Hon'ble Lord Hughes of Ombersley.

Lord Hughes was called to the Bar (Inner Temple) in 1970 and served as a Recorder of the Crown Court from 1985 to 1997. He became a Queen's Counsel in 1990 and was later appointed a judge of the High Court (Family Division from 1997 to 2003; and Queen's Bench Division from 2004 to 2006).

In 2006, he was appointed a judge of the Court of Appeal of England and Wales, serving as the Vice-President of its Criminal Division from 2009 until his appointment as Justice of the Supreme Court in April, 2013.

Lord Toulson

Justice of The Supreme Court, The Right Hon'ble Lord Toulson

Lord Toulson was called to the Bar (Inner Temple) in 1969 and became a bencher in 1995. He became a Queen's Counsel in 1986 and served as a Recorder of the Crown Court from 1987 to 1996. In 1996, he was appointed to the High Court (Queen's Bench Division). He sat in the Commercial Court and in the Administrative Court and was Presiding Judge on the Western Circuit from 1997 to 2002.

Between 2002 and 2006, Lord Toulson was Chairman of the Law Commission of England and Wales, after which he was appointed to the Court of Appeal of England and Wales in 2007. He has also served on the Judicial Appointments Commission for England and Wales.

Lord Toulson was appointed Justice of The Supreme Court in April, 2013.

Lord Hodge

Justice of The Supreme Court, The Right Hon'ble Lord Hodge

Lord Hodge was admitted to the Faculty of Advocates in 1983 and appointed a Queen's Counsel in 1996. From 1997-2003, he was a part-time Law Commissioner at the Scottish Law Commission.

Prior to his appointment to the Supreme Court in April, 2013, Lord Hodge was the Scottish Judge in Exchequer Causes and one of the Scottish Intellectual Property Judges. He was also a Judge in the Lands Valuation Appeal Court and a Commercial Judge.

Lord Hodge joined The Supreme Court in October, 2013 as one of the two Scottish Justices.

PART XI

CHAPTER I

President Dr. Rajendra Prasad administers the oath of office to Sir Harilal J. Kania as the Chief Justice of India, as C. Rajagopalachari, the last Governor General of India, looks on.

CHAPTER II

HON'BLE 1ST JUDGES OF SUPREME COURT OF INDIA

Hon'ble Mr. Justice Harilal Jekisundas Kania

Former Chief Justice of India

DATE OF APPOINTMENT	DATE OF APPOINTMENT AS C.J.I	HELD OFFICE TILL
26-1-1950	26-1-1950	6-11-1951

PROFILE

The Hon'ble Sir Harilal Jekisundas Kania, Kt. Cr. 1943; Chief Justice of India 14th August, 1947-5th November, 1951; son of Jekisundas mother 1925, Kusum, daughter of Sir Chunilal Mehta q.v; one d. Educ B.A. Samaldas College, Bhavnagar; LL.B. Government Law College, Bombay; passed the High Court Advocate (O.S.) Examination 1915. Judge High Court, Bombay. 1933-46, acting Chief Justice in 1944 and 1945; Judge; Federal Court 20th June, 1946 – 13th August, 1947. Retired on 6-11-1951.

FORMER JUDGES OF SUPREME COURT OF INDIA

- **Hon'ble Sir Syed Fazl Ali**

  [Date of Appointment: 26-1-1950 - Held Office till: 18-9-1951]

  Former Judge, Federal/Supreme Court (9-6-1947 to 18-9-1951),

  Judge Supreme Court (15-10-1951 to 30-5-1952)

PROFILE

The Hon'ble Sir Syed Fazl Ali, Kt. (Jan., 1941) B.A. (Allahabad), Bar-at-Law, Judge, Federal Court/Supreme Court-9 Jun. 1947-19 Sept., 1951 and 15th Oct., 1951-30 May, 1952. b. Sept., 19, 1886, son of Saiyid Nazir Ali, mother Kubra Begum, two c. and three d. Educ.: London Mission School, Benaras, Queens College, Benaras, Muir Central College, Allahabad; Middle Temple, London, Practised as a Barrister at Chapra and Patna, Judge, Patna High Court April, 1928, acted as Chief Justice 1938; deputed by the Government of Bihar to settle certain industrial disputes at Jamshedpur. Appointed Permanent Chief Justice January, 1943, Chairman R.I.N. Mutiny Enquiry Commission, April, 46. Member Calcutta Disturbances Enquiry Commission September, 1946; went as Delegate for India to the 2nd Session of the U.N. General Assembly at New York September, 1947; Elected Chairman of the Fifth Committee of the Assembly during that session; Governor at Orissa 1952-54, Chairman, States Reorganization Commission (SRC) 1954-55, Governor Assam, 1956-1959.

BIJAN KUMAR MUKHERJEE (1950-56)

B.K.Mukherjee's family home was Nabadwip in West Bengal, but his birth on 15th August, 1891 took place in Hooghly, Hooghly district, at the home of a maternal uncle, as per the Bengali tradition.

He was the eldest son of Rakhal Das Mukherjea, a Sanskrit Scholar who was also a practicing lawyer at the Chinsura-Hooghly District Courts. His father was more the former than the latter and the family enjoyed high social status but little economic security. Mukherjea was one of a very small number of SCI judges born in what can be termed humble economic circumstances. He had to struggle and can be described as a self-made man.

Mukherjea earned five degrees. He received a BA in Sanskrit and History from Hooghly College in 1912 and an MA in History form Calcutta University in 1914. In the same year, he earned the BL from University Law College, followed by an ML earned at the same institution in 1916. An interest in international law led to a dissertation entitled Problems of Aerial Law, which earned him a Doctor of Law degree in 1923 from Calcutta University. These years of study were filled with many honours. He won gold medals by finishing first in his BL and ML examinations, and also won the Anath Deb Research Prize.

He began the practice of law as an advocate of the Calcutta High Court at age twenty-two on 9th January, 1914. Although in time he would enjoy a successful practice, at the beginning he had a difficult time and to meet expenses he became a part-time lecturer at the University Law College, earning

Rs. 100 per month. Two decades later, in 1934, he was appointed Junior Government Pleader. After briefly officiating as Senior Government pleader, he was appointed an additional Judge of the Calcutta High Court on 9th November, 1936. Aged forty-five then, this appointment was made permanent on 3rd July, 1939. In 1947, he served on the Bengal (Redcliffe) Boundary Commission.

After twelve years on the Calcutta Bench, by which time he was second in seniority, CJI Kania invited Mukherjea to join the federal Court. On 14th October, 1948, at age fifty-seven, he became the first Bengal member of that Court, ending an association with the Calcutta High Court that had spanned a third of a century.

On 23rd December, 1954, I upon CJI Mahajan's retirement, Mukherjea became the fourth CJI. Soon, however, his health began to fail and in late 1955 he was compelled to be on leave for several months. He was to have served as CJI until August, 1956, but declining health forced him to resign on 31st January, 1956.

By virtually all accounts, Mukherjea was among the most brilliant and scholarly of SCI Judges. His The Hindu Law of Religious and Charitable Trusts revealed his extensive knowledge of Hindu law and became a widely read classic. Mukherjea was also named a fellow of Calcutta University. An acclaimed student of Sanskrit, the titles of Bidyaranjan and Saraswati were conferred upon him by the Bangiya Bibhuda Janani Sabha of Nabadwip, a prominent seat of Sanskrit education. He also served as the president of the Bengal Sanskrit Association, and was active in a number of Calcutta literary and cultural organizations, including the Gita Sava and the Sahitya Parishad. His other interests were as diverse as English poetry and the promotion of the Boy Scouts movement in Bengal.

On 22nd February, 1956, three weeks after his worsening heart ailment had compelled to resign from the SCI, Mukherjea died at age sixty-four.

[From the book Judges of the Supreme Court of India (1950-1989) by George H. Gadbois JR]

Hon'ble Mr. Justice Mehr Chand Mahajan

(Former Chief Justice of India)

DATE OF APPOINTMENT	DATE OF APPOINTMENT AS C.J.I	HELD OFFICE TILL
26-1-1950	4-1-1954	22-12-1954

PROFILE

• The Hon'ble Mr. Mehr Chand Mahajan, Chief Justice, Supreme Court of India, 4th January, 1954 to 22nd December, 1954. born December 23rd, 1889. Practised as Lawyer at Dharamshala, 1913; at Gurdaspur, 1914-18; at Lahore, 1918-43; Press, High Court Bar Association, Lahore 1938-43; Director, Punjab National Bank, 1933-43; Fellow and Syndic, Punjab University, 1940-47; Syndic, East Punjab University, 1947-50; Hon. Degree of LL.D., Punjab University; 1948 Pres. D.A.V. College, Managing Committee, 1938-43 All India Fruit Products Assoc., Bombay Session, 1945; Member, Fruit Development Board, Punjab, Judge, Lahore High Court, 1943; Member, R.I.N. Mutiny Commission, 1946; Punjab Boundary Commission, 1947; Judge, East Punjab High Court, 1947, Prime Minister; Jammu and Kashmir State 1947-48; Constitutional Adviser to His Highness the Maharaja of Bikaner, 1948, Judge Federal Court/Supreme Court 4th October, 1948 – 3rd January, 1954.

• Retired on 22-12-1954.

Hon'ble Mr. Justice Sudhi Ranjan Das

(Former Chief Justice of India)

DATE OF APPOINTMENT	DATE OF APPOINTMENT AS C.J.I	HELD OFFICE TILL
26-1-1950	1-2-1956	30-9-1959

PROFILE

The Hon'ble Mr. Sudhi Ranjan Das, born 1st October, 1894, Chief Justice of India 1st February, 1956 to 30th September, 1959; elder son of late Rakhal Chandra Dass; mother 12th May, 1919. Swapna 2nd Daughter of late Rai Bahadur S.B. Majumdar; sons 2 Wg. Cdr Suranjan and Suhrid Ranjan, daughter 1, Anjana. Educ.: Tagore's School, Shanti Niketan, Bangbasi College, Calcutta, University College, Law Graduate Calcutta University, 1915, LL.B. (Lond.) 1st Class first, 1918, called to Bar Gray's Inn 1918; joined Calcutta 1919, Lecturer University Law College; Additional Judge, Calcutta High Court, 1942 *Puisne* Judge, Calcutta High Court since 1944, Chief Justice, Punjab High Court from 19th January, 1949 to 19th January, 1950. Judge Federal Court/Supreme Court of India since 20th January, 1950. Acting Chief Justice of India, 5th September, to 31st October, 1955, 1st December, 1955 to 31st January, 1956. Retired on 30-9-1959.

Mundakulathur Patanjali Sastri (1950-54)

M.P. Sastri, the first judge appointed to the Federal Court after British rule ended, was born in Madras, Tamil Nadu, on 4th January, 1889. His father, Krishna Sastri, was the Senior Sanskrit Pandit at Pachaiyappa's College in Madras. M.P. Sastri was the first member of the family to enter the legal profession.

He received his BA degree, from Pachaiyappa's College in about 1910, and won the Godavatri Sanskrit Scholarship. After teaching briefly at the high school level, Sastri, in about 1912, earned the BL degree from Madras Law College.

He enrolled as an advocate of the Madras High Court in 1914. Early in his career, he gained a reputation of having special expertise in tax law, particularly in the complicated types of tax cases involving Chettry Clients. Shortly after the enactment of the Income-Tax Act, 1922, the Central Government acknowledged his expertise by appointing him Standing Counsel to the Commissioner of Income Tax, a post he held until he was appointed a Judge.

On 15th March, 1939, at age fifty, Sastri became judge of the Madras High Court, replacing his close friend Sir Srinivasa Varadachariar who had been appointed to the Federal Court. Nearly nine years later on 6th December, 1947, by which time he was third in seniority, he became a member of the Federal Court. Fifty-eight at this time, he filled the seat vacant after the resignation of Chief Justice Spens a few months earlier. Sastri served during the remainder of the Federal Court's existence.

Older than CJI Kania, he could not have anticipated becoming CJI. But when death removed Kania from the Bench on 6th November, 1951, Sastri, the most senior associate judge, was named Acting Chief Justice on 7th November. There was then no convention that an outgoing CJI be replaced by the most senior associate judge but Sastri was confirmed as CJI. After having presided over the Court for twenty-six months, he reached retirement age on 4th January, 1954.

He was active with the Delhi branch of the International Law Association, served as Chairman of the Airlines Compensation Commission which dealt with matters concerning the nationalization of airlines, and was a member of the Board of Directors of the Press Trust of India. From 22nd July, 1958 to 20th April, 1962, he was a nominated member of the Madras Legislative Council. At the time of his death on 16th March, 1963 at age seventy-four, he was an active member of the executive council of Banaras Hindu University.

[From the Book Judges of the Supreme Court of India (1950-1989)] by George H. Gadbois JR.

CHAPTER III

FIRST ATTORNEY-GENERAL OF INDIA

MOTILAL C. SETALVAD

Motilal C. Setalvad was born on 12th November, 1884. His father's family had a great deal to do with law. His great-grandfather, Ambashankar, was the Principal Sadar Amin at Ahmedabad and acquired a great reputation as a Judge.

He was admitted to Wilson High School, which was a missionary school and studied therefor seven years till he passed his matriculation examination in 1899. His father was a member of the Bombay Municipal Corporation, fellow of the Bombay University and an elected member of the Bombay Legislative Council. His father conducted the Tilak sedition trial of 1897. He joined college in 1900 and during his college days he passed his B.A. examination in 1904. He passed his LLB examination in 1906. He joined the examination for being admitted as an Advocate on the original side and passed the same on 23rd March, 1911.

Few are able to count their blessings in the space of a single lifespan. Motilal did Advocate-General of Bombay (from 1937 to August 1942), Member of the Indian Delegation to the General Assembly of the United Nations (1947 to 1949) and delegate for India to the Security Council when it took up the Kashmir Issue (1948); then India's first Attorney-General (a Constitutional Office held for a continuous period of twelve years), Chairman of the first Law Commission (1954), President of the Supreme Court Bar Association (1950 to 1968), Founder President of the Bar Association of India from 1959, Nominated Member of the Rajya Sabha (1966). He was awarded Padma Vibhushan on 29-10-1957.

(Fali S. Nariman in the Introduction of the Book My Life Law & Other Things-Motilal C. Setalvad)

•••